The Sex-Role Cycle

Socialization from Infancy to Old Age

Project Staff

SUE DAVIDSON, *Editor*

MERLE FROSCHL, *Field-Testing Coordinator*

FLORENCE HOWE, *Director*

ELIZABETH PHILLIPS, *Editor*

SUSAN TROWBRIDGE, *Design and Production Director*

ALEXANDRA WEINBAUM, *Teaching Guide Editor*

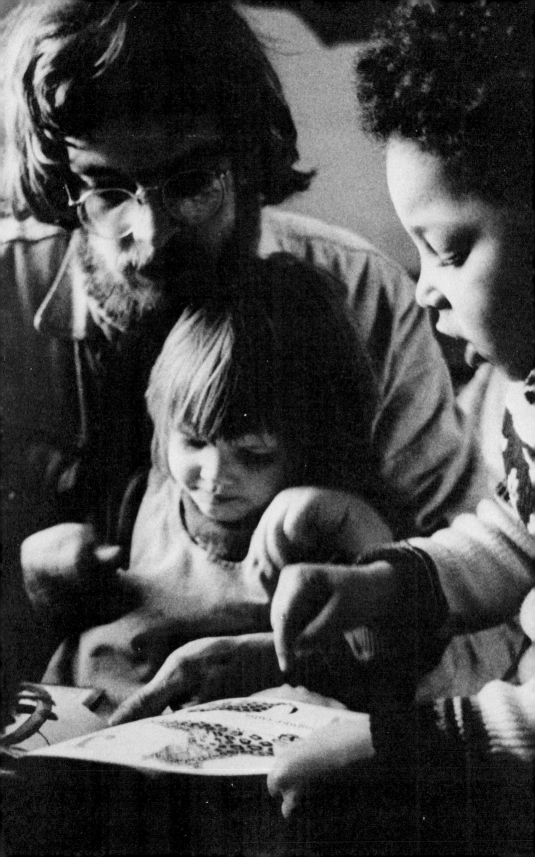

The Sex-Role Cycle

Socialization from Infancy to Old Age

Nancy Romer
BROOKLYN COLLEGE OF THE CITY UNIVERSITY OF NEW YORK

The Feminist Press
OLD WESTBURY, NEW YORK

The McGraw-Hill Book Company
NEW YORK, ST. LOUIS, SAN FRANCISCO

Photo Research by Flavia Rando

**Library of Congress
Cataloging in Publication Data**

Romer, Nancy.
    The sex-role cycle.

    Includes bibliographical references and index.
    1. Sex role. 2. Socialization. 3. Life cycle, Human. I. Title.
HQ1075.R65   305.3   80-17211
ISBN 0-912670-69-X (Feminist Press)
ISBN 0-07-020425-X (McGraw-Hill)

The findings and conclusions of this volume do not necessarily represent the views of the National Endowment for the Humanities.

Table of Contents

Publisher's Acknowledgments

EARLY IN 1973, Mariam Chamberlain and Terry Saario of the Ford Foundation spent one day visiting The Feminist Press on the campus of the State University of New York, College at Old Westbury. They heard staff members describe the early history of The Feminist Press and its goal—to change the sexist education of girls and boys, women and men, through publishing and other projects. They also heard about those books and projects then in progress; they felt our sense of frustration about how little we were able to do directly for the classroom teacher. Advising us about funding, Terry Saario was provocative. "You need to think of yourselves," she said, "in the manner of language labs, testing and developing new texts for students and new instructional materials for teachers." Our "language" was feminism, our intent to provide alternatives to the sexist texts used in schools. The conception was, in fact, precisely the one on which the Press had been founded.

Out of that 1973 meeting came the idea for the *Women's Lives / Women's Work* project. This project, which would not officially begin for more than two years, has allowed us to extend the original concept of The Feminist Press to a broader audience.

We spent the years from 1973 to 1975 assessing the need for a publication project, writing a major funding proposal, steering it through two foundations, negotiating with the Webster Division of McGraw-Hill, our co-publisher. We could not have begun this process without the advice and encouragement of Marilyn Levy of the Rockefeller Family Fund, from which we received a planning grant in 1973. For one year, Phyllis Arlow, Marj Britt, Merle Froschl, and Florence Howe surveyed the needs of teachers for books about women, reviewed the sexist bias of widely used history and literature texts, and interviewed editorial staffs of major educational publishers about their intentions to publish material on women. The research accumulated provided a strong case for the grant proposal first submitted to the Ford Foundation in the summer of 1974.

During the winter of 1974—75, Merle Froschl, Florence Howe, Corrine Lucido, and attorney Janice Goodman (for The Feminist Press) negotiated a co-publishing contract with McGraw-Hill. We could not have proceeded without the strong interest of John Rothermich of McGraw-Hill's Webster Division. Our co-publishing agreement gives control over editorial content and design to The Feminist Press; McGraw-Hill is responsible for distribution of the series to the high school audience, while The Feminist Press is responsible for distribution to colleges, bookstores, libraries, and the general public.

In the summer of 1975, the final proposal—to produce for co-publication a series of twelve supplementary books and their accompanying teaching guides—was funded by the Ford Foundation and the Carnegie Corporation. Project officers Terry Saario and Vivien Stewart were supportive and helpful throughout the life of the project. In 1978, The Feminist Press received funds from the National Endowment for the Humanities to help complete the project. Additional funds also were received from the Edward W. Hazen Foundation and from the Rockefeller Family Fund.

Once initial funding was obtained, The Feminist Press began its search for additional staff to work on the project. The small nucleus of existing staff working on the project was expanded as The Feminist Press hired new employees. The *Women's Lives / Women's Work* project staff ultimately included six people who remained for the duration of the project: Sue Davidson, Merle Froschl, Florence Howe, Elizabeth Phillips, Susan Trowbridge, and Alexandra Weinbaum. Mary Mulrooney, a member of the project staff through 1979, thereafter continued her work as a free-lance production associate for the duration of the project. We also wish to acknowledge the contributions of Dora Janeway Odarenko and Michele Russell, who were on staff through 1977; and Shirley Frank, a Feminist Press staff member who was a member of the project staff through 1979. Helen Schrader, also a Feminist Press staff member, participated on the project during its first year and kept financial records and wrote financial reports throughout the duration of the project.

The *Women's Lives / Women's Work* project staff adopted the methods of work and the decision-making structure developed by The Feminist Press staff as a whole. As a Press "work committee," the project met weekly to make decisions, review progress, discuss problems. The project staff refined the editorial direction of the project, conceptualized and devised guidelines for the books and teaching guides, and identified prospective authors. When proposals came in, the project staff read and evaluated the submissions and made decisions regarding them. Similarly, when manuscripts arrived, the project staff read and commented on them. Project staff members took turns drafting memoranda, reports, and other documents. And the design of the series grew out of the discussions and the ideas generated at the project meetings. The books, teaching guides, and other informational materials had the advantage, at significant stages of development, of the committee's collective direction.

Throughout the life of the project, The Feminist Press itself continued to function and grow. Individuals on staff who were not part of the *Women's Lives / Women's Work* project provided support and advice to the project: Jeanne Bracken, Brenda Carter, Ranice Crosby, Shirley Frank, Brett Harvey, Frances Kelley, Carol Levin, Kam Murrin, Karen Raphael, Marilyn Rosenthal, Helen Schrader, Nancy Shea, Nivia Shearer, Anita Steinberg, Sharon Wigutoff, and Sophie Zimmerman.

The process of evaluation by teachers and students before final publication was as important as the process for developing ideas into books. To this end, we produced testing editions of the books. Field-testing networks were set up throughout the United States in a variety of schools—public, private, inner-city, small town, suburban, and rural—to reach as diverse a student population as possible. We field tested in the following cities, regions, and states: Boston, Massachusetts; Tampa, Florida; Greensboro, North Carolina; Tucson, Arizona; Los Angeles, California; Eugene, Oregon; Seattle, Washington; Shawnee Mission, Kansas; Martha's Vineyard, Massachusetts; New York City; Long Island; New Jersey; Rhode Island; Michigan; Minnesota. We also had an extensive network of educators—350 teachers across the country—who reviewed the books in the series, often using sections of books in classrooms. From teachers' comments, from students' questionnaires, and from tapes of teachers' discussions, we gained valuable information both for revising the books and for developing the teaching guides.

Although there is no easy way to acknowledge the devotion and enthusiasm of hundreds of teachers who willingly volunteered their time and energies, we would like to thank the following teachers—and their students—with whom we worked directly in the testing of *The Sex-Role Cycle: Socialization from Infancy to Old Age*. In Kansas, David Wolfe, District Social Studies Supervisor, helped to contact the following teachers in the Shawnee Mission school district: Vicki Arndt-Helgesen, Jerry Hollembeak, Warren Knutson, Mike Ruggles, John Seevers, Pat Spillman, Marjorie Webb. In the state of Michigan, Jo Jacobs, Coordinator, Office for Sex Equity in Education—with the assistance of Karla Atkinson and Karen Cottledge—helped to contact the following teachers in schools throughout the state: Jo Ann Burns, Mary Ellen Clery, Frances Deckard, Suzanne du Bois, Karen Fenske, Del Gerhardt, Pat Geyer, Shirley Harkless, Sylvia Lawhorn, Susan McFarland, Lenore Morkam, Bert Montiegel, Florence Pangborn, Rose Riopelle, Judy Rogers, Ruth Valdes, Joan Von Holten. In Minnesota, Don Hadfield, Specialist, Equal Educational Opportunities Section, State Department of Education, helped to contact the following teachers: Sonja Anderson, Edward Bauman, Barbara Braham, Colleen Clymer, Katharine Dumas, Judie Hanson, Sandy Johnson, Maya Jones, Gary Olsen, Kathryn Palmer, Dorothy Rock.

Three times during the life of the *Women's Lives / Women's Work* project, an Advisory Board composed of feminist educators and scholars met for a full day to discuss the books and teaching guides. The valuable criticisms and suggestions of the following people who participated in these meetings were essential to the project: Mildred Alpern, Rosalynn Baxandall, Peggy Brick, Ellen Cantarow, Elizabeth Ewen, Barbara Gates, Clarisse Gillcrist, Elaine Hedges, Nancy Hoffman, Susan Klaw, Alice Kessler-Harris, Roberta Kronberger, Merle Levine, Eleanor Newirth, Judith Oksner, Naomi Rosenthal, Judith Schwartz, Judy Scott, Carroll Smith-Rosenberg, Adria Steinberg, Barbara Sussman, Amy Swerdlow. We also want to express our gratitude to Shirley McCune and Nida Thomas, who acted in a general advisory capacity and made many useful suggestions; and to Kathryn Girard and Kathy Salisbury who helped to develop the teacher and student field-testing questionnaires.

One person in particular whom we wish to thank for her work on *The Sex-Role Cycle* is Flavia Rando for her exhaustive photo research and her unbounded enthusiasm for the job. Indeed, her research unearthed so many excellent photographs that it was with great difficulty that we limited ourselves to the ones that we finally selected for this volume.

Others whom we want to acknowledge are Ruth Adam for restoration of the historical photographs; Hedda Garza, who prepared the index; Miriam Hurewitz, who copyedited the manuscript; Angela Kardovich and Randi Book of McGraw-Hill for administrative assistance; Miriam Weintraub and Les Glass of Weinglas Typography Company for the text composition; and Sara Naison-Phillips and Amanda Nelson, the children whose pictures appear on the cover of this book.

The work of the many people mentioned in these acknowledgments has been invaluable to us. We would also like to thank all of you who read this book—because you helped to create the demand that made the *Women's Lives / Women's Work* project possible.

THE FEMINIST PRESS

Author's Acknowledgments

THIS WORK, like most, is an outgrowth of collective efforts. Thus a number of people, as well as social movements, deserve acknowledgment and gratitude.

The greatest influence on this book has been the women's movement. It has given me the encouragement and purpose for graduate training in psychology and for writing such a book. In particular, friends and activists in the Marxist-Feminist wing of the women's movement have helped me to understand and respect people's need and ability to change the ways the social world limits us, despite the tendency to retreat to the safety of the known, and to understand, as well, how social class and race deeply influence the nature of sex-role socialization.

I would like to thank Sheila Alson, Nancy Holmstrom, Nancy Simon, and Maxine Wolfe for reading parts of the manuscript, offering suggestions and ideas, and, moreover, for their very special friendship and support in the last several years. I would also like to thank Elly Bulkin for helping me to present material from a broader and less biased perspective, and Florence and Jack Weisberg for their comments on the later adulthood chapter. Thanks also to Florence Weisberg and Amy Bromson for typing an often messy manuscript with tight deadlines, and to Hedda Garza for doing an extremely thorough index and for being supportive of the ideas in the book.

This book benefits greatly from my contact with students at Brooklyn College, both in my psychology and women's studies courses. I am grateful to them for sharing their own perceptions and experiences, and for encouraging me to be honest and clear.

Elizabeth Phillips has been a most extraordinary editor. Her ideas as well as her tact and kindness have helped shape this book from its start. She has been central in producing a book I am proud of.

Peter Romer-Friedman, my son, deserves a special acknowledgment. His conception, gestation, birth, and infancy all occurred during the writing of this book. Peter has taught me more about my real ideas on human nature, sex roles, and love than anyone else. The loving care he received from Victoria Jamieson freed me to write; I thank her for her intelligence, competence, and affection. I want to thank my sister, Susan Romer-Kaplan, for helping me to get back to writing the book after my child was born. It is particularly gratifying to be able to share our academic interests as well as our sisterly love.

Finally, I want to thank Lew Friedman for being loving and supportive throughout this project in particular and in our lives in general. He has read several drafts of this manuscript and offered important suggestions for improving it. We have tried, with some success, to create a family that is not limited by traditional sex roles and hierarchy, but rather is based on love, mutual respect, and individual needs. As this book explains, however, change on such an individual level cannot be fully successful without changes in the social structure.

NANCY ROMER

Introduction

HUMAN BEINGS ARE PROFOUNDLY SOCIAL. They are deeply influenced by and involved with other people. All people throughout history share a common biological heritage. Yet groups of people differ—from one historical period to another, from one geographical area to a neighboring one, from one racial or ethnic group to another, from one sex to the other. Most of these differences occur because of differing social conditions or environmental influences. People are adaptable and learn to modify their behavior, thoughts, feelings, and attitudes according to the requirements of their culture. Every society trains its young to function within its own view of the world and according to the rules and regulations that control that world. Every society tries to raise its young so that they will accept the ideas and values of that society. The name given to this process that insures the next generation's adherence to the society's ideas and values is socialization.

The process of socialization occurs in almost every human social experience. People are socialized from the moment of birth until the moment of death, at home, at work, at school, at play, with friends, family, and strangers. Individuals do not consciously choose to have most of their socialization experiences; they are simply provided for all people. Yet the individual being socialized should not be viewed simply as a victim of the society. Most people eagerly participate in the process of socialization: they want to fit in, to be like other people in their social world. This is especially true of children who are constantly trying to make sense of the world around them. Most children do not cast judgments on their socialization experiences as much as they willingly accept them. It does not take long for people to grow accustomed to the society into which they are born and to monitor their own behavior, thoughts, and feelings so as to be in harmony with their surroundings. In turn, individuals are likely to go on to influence and socialize others as they have been socialized themselves.

If some miraculous time machine could transport you to another century and a totally different society, or if you dropped by parachute onto an island untouched by the industrialized world, would you know how to behave? Would you know what behavior people there considered friendly, hostile, or insulting? Would it be proper to extend a hand, and, if so, to whom? Would you know from whom to seek shelter or food? Would your clothing seem ridiculous? How would you know what to touch and what to avoid touching? And even if you could communicate in a mutually understood language, you might find that most of your social behavior seemed as alien to the strange inhabitants as theirs to you. Probably, you would need to be instructed about proper social behavior if you were to survive. And yet every five-year-old in that society would have already learned how to behave. They would have had five years' worth of socialization to make them part of that society.

Even within a particular nation, significant changes in accept-able and expected social behavior occur over relatively short periods of time. For example, in sixteenth-century France, children were considered small adults. They participated in adult social and even sexual life as if they were full grown.[1] Today, French children have their own separate social world; they attend schools, nurseries, day-care centers, and playgrounds with other children. Certainly these two distinct socialization experiences produce very different kinds of children who will become very different kinds of adults. In our own national experience, prior to about 125 years ago, most Americans believed that white women as well as all people of color were intellectually inferior to white men. Now we know that race and sex do not determine one's intellectual potential. This shift in the rules and beliefs of the society created major changes in self-concepts, opportunities, awareness. In other words, people's socialization experiences changed dramatically.

Socialization experiences in childhood prepare people for the social roles they will be expected to assume as adults. One's social role—a set of expected behaviors and responsibilities—varies depending on social categories such as sex, race, ethnicity, and social class. In almost every society, sex is one of the most basic and important social categories; when sex is discussed as a social category, it can also be called gender.

Sex, of course, is also a biological category. It becomes a social category when a society requires certain behavior of women and men that is not directly attributable to their biological differences. For example, if the only differences in the expected behavior of women and men were that women, and not men, would menstruate, give birth, and nurse children, then sex would be only a biological category. However, almost every society has fashioned a division of labor around sex that goes far beyond childbirth and nursing.

Following from their biological ability to bear and nurse children, women in most societies are expected to be responsible for the care of children. Beyond the expectation that women will nuture their children, variations on sex roles for women and men are truly astounding. Human societies in their many forms and varieties have begun with the biological differences between the sexes and embroidered wholly different definitions of sex roles. A few examples offered by the late anthropologist Margaret Mead will illustrate this point. Mead lived in and studied three primitive societies in New Guinea—all within a 100-mile radius. In one society she found that child rearing was a main activity for men and women alike: all people, regardless of sex, were expected to be nurturant, loving, and warm. In the second society, both women and men were expected to be very aggressive. Violent fights broke out between people regardless of sex, and very little love or nurturance was expected from anyone. The third society Mead studied was typified by women dominating the practical aspects of family and economic life and men controlling the religious and artistic realms. Women in this society viewed the men's frivolity and spirituality with the same affectionate condescension with which a suburban American husband on a TV situation comedy views his wife's shopping spree. Mead's research demonstrates that the definition of sex roles—the *social* role embroidered upon the biological category of sex—is tremendously variable and dependent upon the history, economy, and culture of a given society. Each society defines "natures" or personalities for women and men which are consistent with the sex roles of that society. Each society organizes socialization experiences to prepare its children for their future sex roles.

The goal of this book is to explain the process by which people in the United States are socialized into sex roles. Because this process is quite complex, only the most important aspects of it will be discussed. Sex-role socialization will be analyzed from a developmental view: by looking at the many influences on individuals as they progress from birth through maturity and finally into old age. Each stage of development teaches the changing individual about the requirements and nuances of sex roles. Yet one should not view the process in a linear fashion, supposing that each developmental period helps to build sex roles in equal and similar ways. As children (and later adults) grow and change, their needs, experiences, and ways of organizing their thoughts about the world change as well. Their understanding of the social world in general and of sex roles in particular becomes much more sophisticated and complex. They not only learn directly from those who consciously teach them sex roles, but they also teach themselves through observing the social world around them. Because of a desire to "fit in" to the society, the individual becomes a partner in the process of sex-role socialization. As people mature, growth in cognitive (intellectual) and emotional development gives them new tools with which to teach themselves sex roles. Such growth also provides tools with which to view sex roles critically, and allows some people to consciously deviate from prescribed roles.

Each period of development offers some new and some overlapping individuals and institutions which form the core of the sex-role socialization experience. These individuals and institutions are called "agents" of sex-role socialization. They create the most direct forms of teaching sex roles. Some examples of these "agents" are parents, teachers, family, friends, peers, TV, books, movies, religious institutions, schools, workplaces. Each of these agents exerts a great deal of influence over us, but some agents are more important and influential during certain periods of our lives. For example, infants are almost totally socialized by parents, family, family friends, and child-care personnel, whereas adolescents are more heavily influenced by peers, TV, movies, books, school, and teachers. Each period of the life cycle has its own features, its own dynamics, and its own way of contributing to the individual's sex-role development.

Personal socialization agents, such as parents, siblings, friends, relatives, and teachers, rarely teach sex roles out of maliciousness. By and large these agents of socialization are not trying to capitalize on conformity to sex roles. They teach sex roles so individuals will fit in to the society as it exists today; they teach sex roles out of loving protectiveness and a desire to see their own way of life validated and supported. Many people believe that learning "appropriate" masculine and feminine behavior helps one to be happy and to succeed in the social and economic world. People often fear that unusual behavior or choices make an individual unhappy; happiness and conformity are equated. This is particularly true in relation to issues surrounding sex roles: sexuality, marriage, having children, masculine and feminine appearance. Parents or friends may bemoan the fate of a homosexual man or a lesbian, or of a woman who has decided not to have children, despite the fact that the individual in question is quite happy with her or his life choices.

Not all socialization agents have the individual's happiness in mind, however. For some agents of socialization—particularly the impersonal ones—the individual's health and happiness are not central at all. The main goal of these agents may be to get people to conform so that their behavior can most easily be controlled. Product manufacturers, for example, wish to create large markets of eager consumers to buy products. Clothing manufacturers may do this by encouraging consumers to feel unfeminine, unmasculine, and/or unattractive unless they are wearing the latest fashions. It would thus be in the manufacturer's interests to sponsor TV and magazine presentations which define sex roles in particular ways. Making distinctions between personal and impersonal agents of socialization and understanding the motives behind each is important in understanding the multiple influences on individuals.

Alongside the developmental perspective, this book will examine the economic and social underpinnings of social roles in general and sex roles in particular. This allows one to view the dynamic influences of the social structure on personality and social development of individuals. Thus, proceeding through the life cycle, one can see the preparation for future economic and social roles (in infancy through adolescence), the pressure to perform these specified roles (in young and middle adulthood), and the shifts that come once the economic and social structure no longer requires such participation (in later adulthood). What will emerge is a picture of the individual's increasing adherence to sex roles until they are discovered to be dysfunctional in the middle years and then begin to reverse with advanced age. Examining the social and economic underpinnings of social roles also helps illuminate the reasons for some social class, racial, and ethnic group differences in sex-role socialization.

While sex roles are of great importance, other social categories and social roles are also key in defining a person's socialization experiences. Such social categories as race, ethnicity, or socio-economic level (or social class) affect variations in the specific definition of the sex roles within a particular society. For example, in American society today, a wealthy woman would be socialized to fulfill a different social role as an adult than a poor woman would be. The two would probably have different expectations of the kinds of lives they will lead as adults, and they will have different socialization experiences: one may attend a small, private school, while the other goes to an overcrowded public school; one may take music lessons, and the other may work part-time after school. The wealthy woman may expect to go to college and marry a factory owner, while the poor woman may drop out of school and go to work in that very factory. While one of the women may fully expect to be provided for by the advantaged men in her life, the other may realize that she must provide for herself because the poor economic circumstances of the men and women around her do not offer a cushion for support. These different experiences will help to socialize these two women into very different types of adults.

Looking at differences in the socialization experiences of poor and wealthy people offers a striking contrast which can be instructive. Another contrast—one that involves the vast major-ity of people in our society—is between working-class and middle-class people. While adults from both of these social classes generally work, either in or outside of the home, the types of jobs, educational backgrounds, incomes, social status, and personal control are different for individuals in these two classes. Working-class people often have not attended college, are regularly employed at skilled or semiskilled jobs, and have family incomes close to or below the national average (about

$16,000).[2] Often working-class jobs are heavily supervised and routinized. On the other hand, members of the middle class, coming generally from more affluent homes where they had more economic and educational opportunities, have usually attended college, work at more highly skilled or profession-al/managerial jobs which permit more independence and self-regulation, and have family incomes above the national average.[3] Their different roles in the economy mean that working-class and middle-class individuals will be socialized in somewhat different ways.

Sex-role socialization in the United States today, then, varies from class to class. And, despite the fact that pressure is exerted on individuals of all ethnic and racial groups to assimilate or "fit in" to the mainstream culture, sex-role socialization is culturally diverse as well. For example, Chicanos (as well as other Hispanics) have traditions of "Marianismo," which means viewing the Virgin Mary as a model for women, especially in regard to sexual purity, motherhood, martyrdom, and self-sacrifice. For Chicano men, masculinity is often defined in terms of "machismo," male bravado or power assertion.[4] Machismo has roots in a response to and an identification with the colonial masters who exerted power over the rest of the society. For Asian Americans, definitions of femininity are still based, to some degree, on remnants of the teachings of Confucianism. This philosophy considers females as sharply inferior to males and insists that women be visibly subordinate to men in family, education, employment, and personal relations.[5]

Many ethnic and racial differences do, in fact, tend to disappear once people reach middle-class status. Research has shown that the greatest ethnic or racial group differences occur among poor and working-class people who often retain the closest ties to the experience of their ancestors. Middle-class status offers people a new shared experience and thus serves to homogenize values and behavior.[6] Yet assimilation is not so easily accomplished by racial minorities, and the process itself can engender painful tension within the individual and between the individual and her or his racial group.

In the United States, views of appropriate sex roles exist within all ethnic, racial, and socioeconomic groupings. But these other important social categories create a social context for and a more specific definition of sex roles. Thus, it is important to view individuals within their broadest social context. Some generalizations about the "female role" or the "male role" are important and meaningful because they truly reflect a consistent set of definitions, experiences, and requirements; however, overgeneralizing may result in the loss of much of the reality of sex roles.

The material for this book has been gathered from many fields in the social sciences: psychology, sociology, anthropology, history, economics. These disciplines attempt to explain how humans function both individually and in their varied societies. I have tried to present and interpret the findings of the best of this research.

Prior to the women's movement of the late 1960s and 1970s, little research existed which did not reflect a white, middle-class, male bias—a bias that was part of the ideology of the society. Most researchers have been white, middle-class men, well socialized by years of professional training by others quite like themselves.[7] Unless they are unusually sensitive to issues surrounding sex roles and sexist bias, social scientists are likely to reflect the views of the society at large. They will probably ask questions which they consider important. Often that means that areas primarily associated with women, such as family, marriage, parent-child relations, nurturance, female sexuality, or women's employment, do not get studied as thoroughly as areas associated with men, such as achievement, male employment, competition, and aggression.[8] Researchers are likely to study individuals for whom these issues are also central, namely white, middle-class males. This partly explains why so little research has been done on working-class and poor people and on people from ethnic or racial minorities. Many more studies have involved males than females, and until the last decade, many other studies did not even bother to report on the sex of the individuals being studied.[9]

In recent years, the political women's movement has had its influence on academic women and men and has virtually transformed the study of sex roles. It has changed not only the methodology but the type of interpretation and analysis of data and the use of personal experience as a valid source of information and ideas. In fact, the feminist perspective articulated in this book and in much of the latest research in sex roles could not have been possible without the growth of this important social and intellectual consciousness. This book uses research from the perspective of the new consciousness of sex roles and their grounding in a particular social structure. While the research offered has been critically chosen on the basis of its quality and/or its insight into the sex-role socialization process, this book does not attempt a systematic presentation and critique of social science research methodology.[10] That would require a great deal of discussion that is not germane to the purposes of this book.

Readers of this book, and of other material in the social sciences, are advised to view research with an attitude of healthy skepticism. All research, with or without numbers, requires interpretation, critical understanding, and the "personal litmus test"—the extent to which the information or analysis helps to explain one's own life and experiences. This book attempts to explain the sex-role socialization process throughout the life cycle. It is meant to raise questions and to initiate a discussion of how we can effect personal and social change.

The Sex-Role Cycle

Socialization from Infancy to Old Age

*To Lew Friedman
and Peter Romer-Friedman*

ONE:
Infancy

Is It a Girl or a Boy?

OUR STUDY OF THE DEVELOPING CHILD begins well before it has come into physical existence. First one must view the future parents, people who have themselves gone through many years of

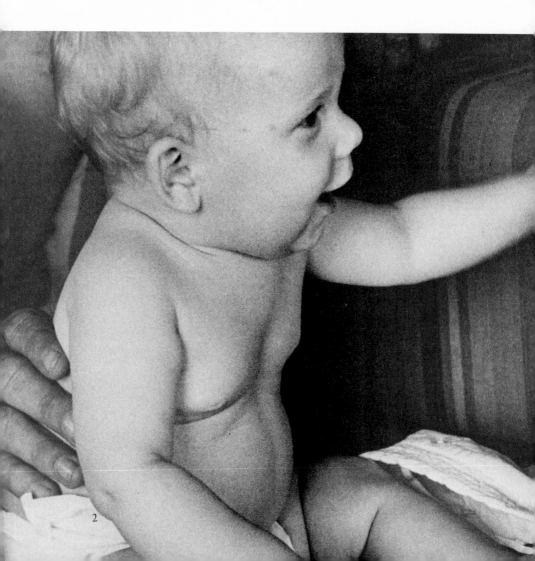

sex-role socialization. They have lived in our culture and probably have accepted the idea that males and females are different, not only physically, but emotionally, intellectually, and socially. When people realize that they are going to have a baby, often they think about what the future baby will be like. Close your eyes and imagine a future child of your own—as an infant, then as a five-year-old, then as an adult. Does that "child" have a sex? Is it female or male? How would the sex of the child change your view of it? Many writers have offered intricate fantasies about their future children that are highly sex-typical, including detailed images of tough, "masculine" boys and delicate, "femi-

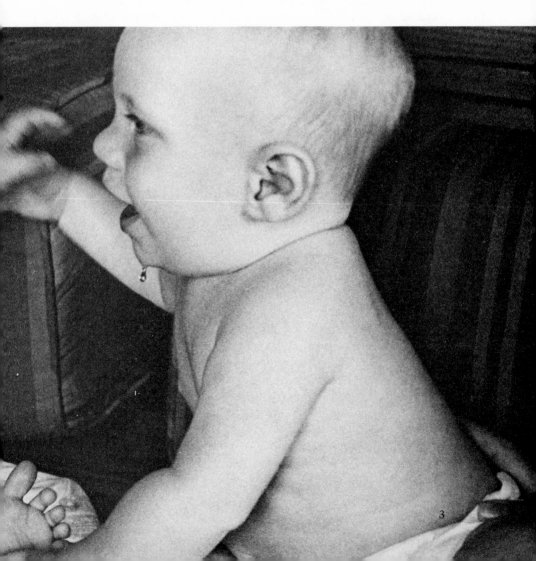

nine" girls.[1] Expectant parents with these views have already started the process of sex-role socialization. Because they anticipate sex-typicality in their babies, they will definitely find it.

After a long, nine-month wait, the baby is finally born. And what is the first question the parents, friends, and relatives ask? "Is it a boy or a girl?" Next they ask if the baby is healthy, how big it is, what its disposition is like.[2] Why is it so important to know the sex of the infant? Since our culture attributes very different characteristics to females and males, knowing a child's biological sex allows us to assign it to a social category. This category helps parents and other people organize their views of the child. These organized views of females and males result in different expectations, different opportunities, different experiences from the moment of birth on.

In one study, mothers and fathers were interviewed within twenty-four hours after the birth of their first child.[3] The parents were individually asked to describe their new babies. Mothers and fathers of boys described their newborns as firmer, larger featured, better coordinated, more alert, stronger, and hardier than the parents of girls described their infants. Mothers and fathers of girls—compared to the boys' parents—were more likely to describe their babies as softer, finer featured, smaller, more inattentive, and more beautiful. But the hospital records showed no objective sex differences between these particular babies in terms of weight, length, muscle tone, irritability, heart or respiratory rates. The parents saw what they expected to see: "typical boys" and "typical girls."

The newborn baby's behavior may not be directly and immediately changed by the views of its parents. However, it is known that adults treat boys and girls differently according to their expectations and that these differences in treatment have profound and long-term effects on the developing child. A number of studies have found that, beginning at birth, parents more often talk to and look at their daughters, while they move their sons' arms and legs more and play more roughly with their sons.[4] Parents tend to stress the social and language aspects of their daughters' development, while emphasizing physical growth in their sons.[5] Although most parents are not aware that they behave differently toward boys and girls, studies show that they do.[6] They treat their babies as individuals, but also as members of a social category.

Biological Sex Differences

Is it possible that adults' behavior toward babies is not only a function of their own cultural definitions of sex, but also a response to innate or inborn sex differences in babies? Researchers do not have all the answers to this complex question. At this point, one can safely say that children are born with some clear and some not-so-clear sex differences, and that these differences may affect the different treatment females and males receive. But the research to date indicates that biological differences alone cannot account for the large variety of sex differences, most of which are grounded in cultural and environmental influences. A brief review of biological sex differences will help us to evaluate the importance of biological influences on the development of sex differences in behavior, thoughts, and feelings.

Most animals, including humans, become male or female upon conception. When the sperm cell from the father fertilizes the egg cell of the mother, each of these cells contributes twenty-three chromosomes (consisting of thousands of bits of genetic material known as genes) to the new human organism. Only one of these twenty-three pairs of chromosomes will determine the sex of the developing fetus. The other twenty-two pairs of chromosomes are not related to the sex of the future individual. All females have two chromosomes referred to as X chromosomes (XX) because when examined under a microscope, they look like the letter X. Males have one X chromosome and one Y chromosome (XY). The Y chromosome is much smaller than the X chromosome and looks like a letter X with its bottom left line missing, hence the label Y. The future offspring receives only one sex chromosome from each parent: from the mother it receives one X chromosome, from the father it receives either a Y or an X chromosome. Whether the developing fetus gets two X chromosomes or an X and a Y chromosome is influenced by the acid level of the mother's vaginal environment. Different acid levels help determine whether a sperm cell carrying an X or a sperm cell carrying a Y is more likely to fertilize the ovum. If the sperm cell that fertilizes the egg contains an X chromosome, the future offspring will be a girl (XX). If the sperm cell contains a Y chromosome, the future individual will be a boy (XY). It is the presence of the Y chromosome that makes the male different from the female embryo. This chromosomal difference is the basic source of physical or biological sex differences.

For the first six to seven weeks of gestation or pregnancy, the male and female human embryos look very much alike. The differences in their chromosomes have not expressed themselves in physical structure. Their gonads—future sex organs— have not begun to differentiate. If the embryo has XY chromosomes, at around eight weeks into the gestation period it begins to manufacture male hormones and develop male genitals and a male reproductive system. If the embryo has XX chromosomes, at around twelve weeks into the gestation period it begins to develop female genitals and a female reproductive system. All human beings start out with the same undifferentiated or general sexual structure. Our sex chromosomes direct the quantity and type of hormones—chemical agents—that in turn determine the development of either a penis or clitoris, ejaculatory ducts or vagina, testes or ovaries. This is how differences in chromosomes create the biologically obvious differences between the sexes.[7]

After the normal nine-month gestation period, the newborn emerges as a fragile bundle of reflexes struggling to survive in a foreign environment. In most ways, the behavior of male and female newborns is alike. They cry when discomforted, startle at loud noises, suck when their mouths are touched by an object, and sleep most of the time. In most families, babies receive love and protection from their relatives and close friends regardless of sex. While the basic behavioral mechanisms of newborn boys and girls are alike, there are some physical differences. The clearest sex differences are in genitals, hormones, and sex chromosomes. Other physical sex differences present at birth are quite small and may only be detected when looking at all males as a group and all females as a group. Differences between individual females and males may be negligible or nonexistent. Newborn females, as a group, are more advanced in bone or skeletal growth.[8] In general, the female is more resistant to disease, less likely to have birth defects, and more likely to survive the birth experience than the male.[9] On the other hand, newborn males, as a group, are somewhat more muscularly developed and are slightly heavier and longer than females. These differences are found by comparing groups of thousands of males and females. Many female newborns are longer, heavier, and more muscularly developed than many newborn males.[10] Using the data on weight to demonstrate the very small differences that are considered to be scientifically significant, one finds the average birth weight of white males to be 7.50 pounds and of white females to be 7.44 pounds.[11]

While there is general agreement that some *physical* differences exist at birth, there is much debate among social scientists as to whether there are *behavioral* sex differences in newborns: differences in vocalization, activity level, irritability, smiling, fear and anxiety, and dependency. Some studies have found sex differences in these areas while other studies have not. Since the evidence is so contradictory, one cannot be sure that major sex differences in behavior exist at birth.[12].

Environmental Influences

A good deal of evidence exists that sex differences in the behavior of infants are present after several months of life and exposure to the social world. One of the reasons for this is that infants' behavior can be altered by slight differences in the environment. Rewards—in the form of pleasurable experiences—can reinforce or encourage certain kinds of behavior, while lack of rewards and unpleasurable experiences can inhibit them.

While newborn males and females do not differ significantly in the amount they vocalize or make voice-related sounds, by four months, the sounds that female infants make are more often linked to exciting, interesting, or changing facets of their environment. Females are also more likely than males to make sounds when they see human faces or humanlike forms. Child psychologist Jerome Kagan suggests that these sex differences in vocalizations may be due to the importance parents place on their daughters' language and social development and the greater amount of time mothers spend talking to and looking at their infant daughters compared to their infant sons.[13] Sex differences in language and social development have been found to persist and diversify with age.[14]

Susan Goldberg and Michael Lewis studied infants when they were six months old and then again when these same infants were thirteen months old.[15] They observed the infants and their mothers in play situations. They were looking specifically for sex differences in the infants' behavior and for differences in mothers' handling of sons and daughters. When the infants were six months old, the researchers found no sex differences in their play behavior. However, mothers of six-month-old girls were more likely to touch, talk to, and handle their infants than were mothers of six-month-old boys. At thirteen months, some sex differences in behavior emerged; boys oriented less of their play toward the mother, they banged toys more often, and played more actively and vigorously compared to the girls. The researchers attributed these sex differences in behavior at thirteen months to the differences they observed in the behavior of the mothers of boys and girls at six months of age. Babies may not change their behavior immediately in response to differential treatment, but they usually do respond in time.

Social scientists know that during early and late childhood, as well as during adolescence, sex differences in two important categories of behavior are maintained: boys tend to be more physically active and athletic and girls tend to be more verbal and sociable.[16] Researchers also know that parents tend to train their sons and daughters differentially. They discipline sons more often via physical punishment, and they stress the importance of sons' physical competence and assertiveness. With daughters, parents discipline with love-oriented techniques such as praise or threats that love will be withdrawn, and they stress language and social skills.[17]

While it is altogether possible and even probable that there is some predisposition toward earlier language development in girls and toward muscular strength in boys, it is clear that these small differences at birth are embroidered upon and extended by the parents, friends, relatives, and general culture. Certain inborn sex differences may be the starting point, but the most dramatic and measurable sex differences are those that emerge with age and differential treatment in a sex-stereotyping world.

Pink and Blue

Most parents arrange their babies' physical environments in ways that increase the likelihood of their being sex-typical. Parents often dress children in sex-typical clothes: their daughters in pink and their sons in blue.[18] In fact, clothes manufactured for infants come in pink, blue, and yellow ("if you don't know the sex of the new baby"). Many parents who would not necessarily choose pink for their daughters and blue for their sons find themselves urged to do so by eager salespeople. Parents who feel committed to buying non-sex-typical clothes for their infants may have to argue with salespeople or buy the more expensive infant clothes that come in a greater variety of colors. Most parents, then, are persuaded to buy the less expensive, pink and blue clothes. These colors and clothes are automatic cues for strangers, friends, and family to behave toward the infant in a fashion that is considered appropriate for the baby's sex. So a female baby in pink bows and frills rouses comments on her cuteness or doll-like qualities. The baby in a little sweat suit with a Yankee emblem is sure to be called "slugger." Girls are permitted greater leniency than boys in wearing some non-sex-typical clothes such as overalls. But parents are pressured, not only by salespeople but by their own parents, relatives, and friends, as well as strangers, to make their infant boys look "masculine." Dressing a son in pink clothes or with frills, let alone in a dress, would clearly meet with strong disapproval.

Parents also give infants sex-appropriate toys and furnish their rooms accordingly. A research team analyzed the contents of the rooms of babies ranging in age from one to twelve months. They found that girls' rooms more often contained dolls (especially baby dolls); stuffed animals; floral decorations; and ruffles. Boys' rooms were more likely to have educational art materials; spatial-temporal objects such as magnets, clocks, and rockets; sports equipment; and nonstuffed toy animals.[19] These sex differences in parents' behavior and expectations, and in the opportunities they thus provide their children, generally yield real differences in the interests and skills developed by boys and girls.

Group Differences

Most people would agree on some general definitions of the social categories of "male" and "female." However, there are also important differences in the way people view males and females, depending on their own sex, ethnicity, and social class. For example, fathers may treat their daughters and sons in different ways than mothers do. Evidence indicates that fathers, who usually spend less time with their children, have more sex-typical views of children than do mothers.[20] This may be due to many fathers' lack of practical experience with children, experience that might decrease their generalizations about sex differences in children. Fathers and mothers, as males and females themselves, respond to the sex categories in different ways. Fathers are more likely to give more leeway to and impose fewer rules on their daughters, while mothers are more lenient with their sons.[21]

Other studies indicate that there may be social class differences in the ways in which parents handle their sons and daughters. Jerome Kagan observed mothers and their children over the span of the babies' infancy. These observations took place both in the families' homes and in the experimenter's laboratory. Kagan noted how mothers handled their babies, how babies responded, and how the babies developed. He found that middle-class women, more than working-class women, encouraged their daughters to learn to speak early, solve problems, and be active in learning experiences. Accordingly, middle-class daughters were more advanced than working-class daughters in the crucial areas of language and intellectual development. These class differences were not as great for boys.[22]

Kagan theorizes that many working-class mothers are fatalistic about their own and their daughters' future and are not confident about training their daughters to be effective and independent adults. Partly because of their low status and the poor job opportunities available to them, working-class women may feel unable to change their environment. The working-class woman may, unknowingly, pass on her sense of powerlessness and low expectations to her daughter by not talking enough with her and by not encouraging an active learning style. This may be at least partly a function of the fewer resources available for raising children in working-class families. By comparison, middle-class women often feel more effective and powerful themselves. They may feel more able to raise their daughters to do well in school and to be independent people. Middle-class mothers may, in fact, have unrealistically high expectations of their daughters.

A mother's social-class background, experiences, and outlook may have a greater influence on daughters than on sons because mothers tend to be more identified with and closer to their daughters. Mothers of all class backgrounds talk to their baby daughters more than to their baby sons. They may see themselves as more similar to their daughters than to their sons; mothers can imagine their daughters' adulthood as an extension of their own. Thus, perhaps more of the mothers' own feelings and expectations are applied to their daughters than to their sons. Since no studies have been done looking at class differences in father-infant interactions, we do not know whether fathers would influence their sons more than their daughters or what the nature of this influence would be.

So far, no studies have compared early parent-infant interactions in families of various ethnic and religious backgrounds. However, since people from different ethnic and religious groups view sex roles somewhat differently, one would expect to find some ethnic and religious variation in the rearing of males and females. In Puerto Rican families, for example, boys appear to be highly valued over girls. In some Puerto Rican families, girl infants are diapered in private while boy infants are proudly diapered in full public view. Since people fit into several social categories at once—for example, a working-class, white, Jewish female or a middle-class, West Indian, Protestant male—they respond to babies and affect them according to the many social influences on them and their differing views of the "male" and "female" categories.

A Classic Study

John Money and his associates have done extensive research on the relationship between chromosomes, hormones, and environmental influences on the sex-role development of children. They have gathered data on children born with conflicting internal and external sexual organs, for example children who have the genetic and internal structures of a male, but the external genitals of a female or vice versa. Some of these children have been shown to have genetic and/or hormonal abnormalities. In some cases, a sex reassignment has been made, and the child has been treated through hormone therapy and/or corrective surgery of the sex organs to make the individual internally and externally consistent. Money stresses the importance of environmental influences in determining the sexual and psychological adjustment of the individual. He has found that, regardless of the genetic and hormonal sex of the child, the most important factor in the child's psychosexual differentiation or development is his or her sex assignment and the sex-distinguishing treatment received from parents and other significant people in the social environment.

Money reports on a case of identical twin boys, one of whom had his penis removed at age seven months as a result of an accident in circumcision. Despite the fact that the child was genetically and hormonally male, the parents, in conjunction with Money's research institute, began a program of sex re-assignment. At seventeen months, the child's name, clothing, and hairstyle were changed. At twenty-one months, the doctors performed genital surgery to create a vagina. They plan to do further genital surgery and begin hormone treatments when the child is full grown. Thus until the child is full grown, she is internally (genetically and hormonally) a male, but externally (genitals and sex assignment) a female. With her male twin to compare her to, this is a perfect test case for the strength of environment over biology. The twins' mother describes how she consciously has raised her children sex-typically. She has dressed her daughter in frilly blouses, often in pink, and let her hair grow long. She dressed her son in pants, often in blue, and cut his hair short. By four and a half years of age, the daughter, according to the mother, was much neater than the son. The parents have instructed the children in their respective sex roles: the daughter has helped her mother with the kitchen chores, while the son has helped his father. By six years of age, the son requested toy cars and a garage as gifts, while the daughter asked for dolls. The son wanted to be a fireman when he grew up, while the daughter hoped to be a teacher. The daughter has been an extremely energetic and often domineering child, but she has been described as an assertive "mother hen," rather than as aggressive in a more typically masculine fashion. Money last reported on the twins when they were nine years old. At that point, the children behaved quite differently: one as a "typical girl," the other as a "typical boy." Yet they were biologically identical: the only differences between them were surgically produced external genitalia for one of them and differential treatment from parents and others.[23]

While such cases are extremely rare, they are important because they help to unravel the multiple effects of biology and environment on the individual.

Women as Child Rearers

Throughout infancy, a baby grows at a rapid rate—physically, intellectually, and emotionally. While most personality theorists agree that the central themes, structure, and dynamics of personality are developed within the first five years of life, a growing number of social scientists are focusing special attention on personality development from birth to age two.

Nancy Chodorow and Dorothy Dinnerstein, in separate but related work, emphasize the impact on personality development of the fact that almost all infants in our society are raised by women (mothers, aunts, grandmothers, nurses, baby-sitters, child-care workers). Women, as sex-role-socialized individuals, perceive their little girls and boys in different ways. Girls are usually seen as closer and more similar to the mother or other female care giver; boys are usually considered more distinct and distant. This is supported in part by Kagan's research on mothers' handling of sons and daughters. Chodorow and Dinnerstein further theorize that infants experience their relationships with their mothers or primary care givers differently depending on whether they are male (and thus distinct from the mother) or female (and thus similar to the mother). Chodorow and Dinnerstein argue that these early experiences have far-reaching influence on the future adult's ability and desire to be close, loving, and nurturant with others (traditionally feminine characteristics) and to be autonomous, independent, and self-defining (traditionally masculine characteristics).[24]

Chodorow's and Dinnerstein's analyses emphasize the great

influence of the social structure—which assigns primary child-care responsibility to women—on the development of human character and personality. Their work also points the way to some of the areas one needs to know more about in order to fully understand sex-role development. So far, no in-depth studies have analyzed the differences in personality that could be expected if a child's primary care giver were a man or if child care were shared equally by a man and a woman or by a group of people of both sexes.

TWO:
Early Childhood

Sizing Up the World

ONCE A BABY BEGINS to use language (at about one and a half to two years), it has reached the period of development called early childhood. This period lasts until age five or six. Based on

infancy experiences, the young child has taken several steps toward becoming sex-typical. By early childhood, some sex differences are found, most probably influenced by differential treatment in infancy. Females' language development is often more advanced than males', and males tend to be more physically active than females.

Using language aids the child in learning about the world. The child's ability to think and comprehend contributes to extremely rapid social development. In infancy, babies' major social tasks were to develop attachments to those closest to them (usually mothers and/or fathers) and to understand that those

who care for them are distinct beings who are emotionally but not physically attached to them. By the time children complete early childhood, at about five or six years of age, they have accomplished many more complex social tasks. They can form friendships or rudimentary play relationships with other children and are able to play for an extended period of time without constant supervision. They comprehend that some people have more power than others and that money (in our society) often translates into power. They understand that the human species is divided into two sexes that are supposed to be very different from each other. Similarly, they begin to comprehend racial categories. As children come to understand sex and race groupings, they learn that males and male-associated activities are more highly valued than females and female- associated activities. They learn, too, that in the United States, whites are more highly valued by the society at large than are people of color.[1]

During early childhood, children generally do not consider alternatives that they do not see directly. Although they may argue and disobey from time to time, they do not challenge the values of the people around them. Their views of the social world are limited, rigid, and confused. They are constantly trying to figure out just how to act, and will seek guidelines for appropriate behavior.[2] Sex roles offer them such guidelines. By about age two, most children know what sex they are, and they can accurately identify other males and females, usually by their clothes and hairstyles. Later in the early childhood period, they come to understand that they will remain the sex they are throughout their lives. Learning that males and females are "different," following the "sex-appropriate" guidelines for social behavior, helps children to feel more comfortable and sure of themselves in social interactions. By about age four, boys and girls usually prefer toys which society deems appropriate for their sex, such as dolls for girls and trucks for boys, although this tendency is stronger for boys than for girls.[3] At this stage, children size up the social world in an extremely stereotypical fashion, and try to fit themselves into it.

Families

The social world around them is also actively trying to get children to adhere to sex roles. Most parents hope their children will behave in "sex-appropriate" ways; and their desires for sex-typicality increase as their children get older.[4] Parents, however, are not all the same, and they teach their children different things about sex roles depending on their beliefs and values, and on the way they live and act. Most children live with their mothers and fathers. Large numbers of children, however, live in different kinds of families. Many live with only their mothers; others live in lesbian or (less frequently) in male homosexual families. Some live in communes or collectives. Within each of these kinds of families, there is great variety. While many mothers work outside the home, some do not. Some fathers take responsibility for child care and housekeeping; others believe this is "women's work." So while generalizations about parents' behavior can help illuminate large patterns, one has to remember that individual parents may not "fit" all the generalizations.

While female and male infants may be treated somewhat differently by their parents, most parents increase their differential treatment of their daughters and sons during early childhood. The activities and experiences parents suggest or choose for their children help create greater differences between girls and boys. When there is enough money in a family for more than one or two bedrooms, sisters and brothers usually sleep in separate rooms. Preschool boys' rooms (decorated and paid for by their parents) are most likely to have sports equipment and pictures; toy cars; paints and clay; and toy animals. Preschool girls' rooms are most likely to have decorative ruffles on beds; dolls; doll houses; and domestic items such as sinks, tea sets, pots and pans.[5]

Arranging different play environments for sons and daughters is one of the many ways parents participate in sex-role socialization. In addition, parents usually expect and permit a good deal more physical aggression and rowdiness—and less

obedience and dependence—in their sons than in their daughters. Most parents also expect their sons to master tasks—such as dressing themselves, going out to play without telling a parent, crossing the street alone, and using sharp tools—at an earlier age than their daughters. Mothers are also more likely to encourage their daughters to follow them around the house and stay close to them, while discouraging their sons from the very same behavior.[6]

Parents usually treat daughters and sons differently because they believe that different behaviors and personalities are required for females and males. Many parents believe that such sex differences are "natural." Most parents think that their differential treatment of their daughters and sons will enable their children to lead healthy and happy lives. Parents have many ways of letting their children know what they believe to be correct behavior. They may tell the children directly or reward them for "appropriate" behavior via compliments, affection, or special favors. Parents may also punish their children for "inappropriate" behavior by hitting, yelling, taking away privileges, or withdrawing affection.

In addition, parents present themselves to their children as role models. They may encourage their sons to imitate many aspects of the father's behavior and want their daughters to imitate their mother's. Children are frequently discouraged from imitating the sex-typical behaviors of their opposite-sex parent, and parents often form special and close relationships with children of their own sex. This may be why many women prefer to have at least one girl baby and many men prefer at least one son.[7] Women and men often expect their same-sex child to be like them, and they may take special pride in the relationship with this child. A father may have his young son hand him carpentry tools, teach his son to catch and throw a ball, or have him help wash the car. A mother may enjoy having her daughter dress up in her oversized clothes, put on Mommy's makeup, or help to sweep the floor with a miniature broom. When children act like their same-sex parents, they are likely to get approval ("just like Daddy" or "just like Mommy") from both their parents. The physical similarity, the common sex category, and the special affection makes a same-sex parent a likely model for a child to imitate in his or her own social behavior.

In a longitudinal study, Jerome Kagan and Howard Moss studied a large group of children and their families from birth until adulthood.[8] Kagan and Moss were interested in finding out what parent behaviors seemed to influence children to achieve, both at school and later at work. They examined the subjects who were most achievement-oriented as adults and traced back their relationships with their mothers when they were pre-schoolers. They found that males who were achievers as adults usually had very close and loving relationships with their mothers from birth to three years of age, while female achievers were likely to have "cooler," more distant relationships with their mothers. Unfortunately, Kagan and Moss did not collect data on these subjects' relationships with their fathers, so they did not consider the influence of father-child relationships on these children's achievement behavior. A decade later, Lois Hoffman suggested that the achievement-oriented girls in the Kagan and Moss study did not actually have cold relationships with their mothers, but perhaps did not experience "smother love" and so were trained to be less dependent on a same-sex parent. She also suggested that mothers who have activities and interests beside that of mothering may offer their daughters less traditional sex-role models. Having a slight separation between mother and daughter may allow for less sex-typicality and, therefore, more achievement orientation in adulthood. On the other hand, unusually supportive relationships with mothers in early childhood may facilitate achievement (which is consistent with the male sex role) for males.[9]

The way in which work is divided among family members offers a potent sex-role model to sons and daughters. Due to traditional beliefs about sex roles, a common need for dividing up the labor in a family, and the fact that men are usually paid quite a lot more for their employment than are women, many children in our society grow up with a mother at home, taking care of children, husband, and house, and a father working outside the home for pay. However, over 40 percent of all preschool children and 65 percent of school-age children have mothers who work outside the home. This family pattern is becoming more common. In addition, in many families women provide the primary income for the family—approximately one in every four households is headed by a woman. In other families, children may be financially supported by both parents or by the father only, but may live with the mother.

Studies on the role of the father and the effects on children of his absence (due to divorce or death) have been plagued with a desire to preserve the ideal of the traditional nuclear family with mom at home, dad at work, and kids happily at play. Research on the effects of a mother's employment on children has been similarly biased. Until the recent wave of new research, families that did not conform to this supposed ideal standard were often considered deviant or abnormal. Studies of these families often suffered from a lack of specificity and serious analysis. In truth, the "ideal" nuclear family model can no longer be considered the norm: the majority of American children do not live in families with mother at home with the children and father working for pay.[10] It is therefore crucial to take a serious look at other forms of family life.

Having a mother who is employed outside the home and a father who does household tasks encourages children to be less sex-typical. A less traditional role model for a mother or father allows a child to see alternatives to the "little woman at home" and the "all-powerful male provider." Children in such homes tend to be somewhat less sex-typical in their own activities and in their views of appropriate behavior for adult males and females.[11] However, even when parents are not sex-typical in their own behavior and the behavior they encourage in their children, most of their preschool children are, nonetheless, fairly sex-typical. This is due to several factors. Parents are not the only influence on children's social views. Television, peers, other family members, neighbors, and books also show young children what is "typical" and "normal" in the world. Eager to "fit in," children often follow these other clearly delineated sex roles. The rigid roles may be easier for young children to understand than the blended and more complex version of sex roles offered by their nontraditional parents. And if the preschool child perceives that most of the rest of the world is divided into "male" and "female" domains, having nontraditional parents does not exempt the child from wanting to fit into these neat categories. In addition, almost all parents, including those who are nontraditional, behave in some sex-typical ways and encourage some sex-typical behavior in their children as well. This may not be planned, and the parents may be unaware of what they are doing. Sex roles are so pervasive in our society that it is hard to be conscious of all the ways that individuals are influenced by them. The real influence of nontraditional parents usually comes later in the child's life when she or he may be more able to understand and appreciate the complexity of the social world.

What about the millions of children raised in one-parent families? Will they become "normal" males or females? Researchers have found that it is not necessary to have both a female and male parent (or parent figure) present for healthy psychosexual development. Most of the research has been done on children whose fathers are absent. This is partly because in our culture the major role of child care has been assigned to females. Thus, in a marital separation or divorce, the mother is most often the parent who lives with and raises the children. Also, female life expectancy is longer, and so most one-parent families due to the death of a parent also consist of the mother and children.

Boys whose fathers are absent can learn about the male role through examples provided by neighbors, friends, and television, and will be rewarded for male sex-typical behavior by mothers and others.[12] However, some researchers have found these boys to be somewhat more likely to have difficulty in developing a masculine identity fully independent of the mother.[13] Some single mothers are extremely sensitive to the problems their sons may face in father-absent homes, and may overcompensate by heavily encouraging masculine behavior in their sons and by providing adult male friends as models. This can lead to an extremely masculinized style of behavior in boys from father-absent homes.[14]

Until adolescence, girls whose fathers are absent appear to be quite similar to girls whose fathers live with them. During adolescence, however, relationships with male peers appear to be more central to the social and psychological lives of girls from father-absent homes. Some difficulties in establishing satisfying relationships with males have been reported.[15] These studies indicate the importance and potential influence of a loving father's presence and participation in the rearing of children. However, his absence will not necessarily spell trouble for his sons or daughters. Much depends on how the mother raises the children. In addition, the presence of a hostile or abusive father (or mother) may be extremely damaging to the children.[16] The best of all possible child-rearing circumstances seems to be multiple loving and available parent figures, contact with both males and females of many ages, and a variety of role models for the child.

Parents are not the only family members who influence children. A child is likely to be less sex-typical if she or he has a sibling of the opposite sex.[17] This is due to the fact that a child with an opposite-sex sibling has the opportunity to observe the sibling and play with her or his toys. A younger sister may be brought along to a kickball game with her big brother if an extra player is needed. A boy may play house with his sister and her friends if they need a baby or a father. So siblings, too, teach each other sex roles.

Television

During early childhood, girls and boys encounter the broader social world in the form of mass media, nursery or preschool programs, and children other than siblings. Almost all American children have access to television. The U.S. Surgeon General's report indicates that preschool children spend more of their waking hours watching TV than they spend in any other single activity. Average TV viewing time for preschoolers is three to five hours daily. Thus the influence of television is potentially very great. A number of child psychologists believe that excessive TV viewing helps to create a passive style of learning because there is no real interaction between the child and the performers. Children may sit for hours staring, trancelike, without actively exploring the world around them.[18] Aside from fostering passive learning, TV programs usually have a set of values and beliefs that they present to children in an action-packed, highly stylized, and repetitive fashion. These values almost always include adherence to traditional sex roles.

Sarah Sternglanz and Lisa Serbin surveyed the ten most popular (according to Neilsen ratings) children's TV shows to analyze the ways in which males and females are portrayed on television.[19] Four of the top ten shows had to be eliminated because they contained *no* regular female characters, human or animal. On the six remaining "most popular" shows, most of the characters (67 percent) were male. Male characters were more often portrayed as aggressive, constructive, or as problem solvers, while female characters were more often portrayed as deferential, or as witches or magical creatures. Females were more frequently punished for high levels of activity. Sternglanz and Serbin concluded that males and females were not only unequally visible on TV, but were also portrayed quite differently. Even specifically educational shows such as Sesame Street have been criticized for having too few females and some sex-stereotypical roles.[20]

When children watch TV, they also watch commercials that try to sell them many products. Having very little conception of how much things cost or of how much money their parents have, preschool children often want to buy what they see advertised on television. Most manufacturers have done research on what types of advertising and packaging will get people to buy their products. They have learned that pictures of males on box tops of toys are not only attractive to boys and their parents, but to girls and their parents as well. Toys with pictures of girls on the box tops are usually bought only by or for girls. Thus, sex-neutral toys, such as games, books, puppets, and science and craft sets, are usually packaged with pictures of boys on them, and sometimes, but not usually, with boys and girls. They are never packaged with pictures of girls only.[21] On television, boy models play with erector sets, athletic equipment, trucks, and trains, while girl models try out baby dolls, carriages, and tea sets. Advertisers and toy manufacturers are trying to make money, and they play on children's desire to be appropriate males or females. In doing so, they contribute to the process of sex-typing children by defining what is available and what is sex-appropriate.

Children who watch "adult" TV are exposed to even stronger images of sex-appropriate items and values. Lucy Komisar describes the portrayal of adult women in TV commercials as unintelligent, childlike, only interested in home and family, and unconcerned about the world of employment or non-home-related creativity.[22] Even when commercials try to appeal to the woman who works outside of the home (the majority of all women), the emphasis is usually placed on her beauty or her nurturing qualities. Komisar insists that advertisers do not create these images of women or men, but rather they reflect views or stereotypes already existing in the society. Since young children believe that television tells the truth, they may think that "the truth" involves extreme versions of sex roles. In the search for appropriate social behavior, children are likely to internalize these views and adopt these sex-typical behaviors.

Formal Preschool Training

Lessons of traditional sex roles are also taught in formal preschool settings, be they child-care centers, nursery schools, or Head Start programs. Often these lessons are not planned or even consciously presented by teachers or child-care workers, adults who usually share the sex-role stereotypes of the culture. One observational study of nursery school classrooms indicated that teachers rewarded girls primarily for feminine sex-typed activities such as playing with dolls and doll houses, painting and art work, playing in the kitchen, and quietly listening to stories. They rewarded boys mainly for masculine sex-typed activities such as playing with building blocks and transportation toys, riding tricycles, and climbing.[23] Another observational study of a nursery school with an explicitly open sex-role policy showed that girls were more often complimented for their good looks than were boys. Special praise was given to girls if they wore dresses to school, despite the fact that dresses restrict the free movement crucial to preschool children's play.[24]

Lisa Serbin describes her visit to a nursery school:

I watched during music time, and the first thing I saw was the teacher asking the little boys to stand up while "Here Comes Peter Cottontail" was played on the piano. All the boys were bunnies. They hopped all over the room. After the boys had had their turn and had all been Peter Cottontail, they sat down, and then it was the girls' turn.

This time the teacher played the Easter Parade song, "In Your Easter Bonnet. . ." The girls paraded around the room. At the end,the teacher at the piano stood up and looked very solemn. She said, "Ladies, that isn't the way we have a parade. When we have a parade, we all walk very nicely, and we pick up our feet so we don't make lots of noise on the floor, and we all walk like little ladies. Now let's do it again." She sat down and played "In Your Easter Bonnet" again, and the little girls went very quietly tiptoeing around the room. Then they sat down.

A little boy raised his hand and said, "The girls got to go twice. Don't we get to go twice?" The teacher sat down at the piano and played "Here Comes Peter Cottontail." The boys hopped all over the room and made quite a good bit of noise, but nobody said anything to them about being "gentlemanly" or quiet or making "nicely" restrained movements.[25]

Serbin and her colleagues also observed a nursery school classroom in which children were making paper baskets that needed to be stapled. The teachers generally did the stapling for the girls, while they offered instructions to the boys on how to staple their baskets by themselves. These teachers were showing the children that boys can do more grownup, difficult, and dangerous tasks, while girls are still dependent upon the help of others.[26]

Carole Joffe and Barbara Harrison, in separate studies, report that even within a school with a nontraditional sex-role policy, educational materials that offer alternatives to traditional sex roles are rare. They are difficult to find because they are not widely produced.[27] In a review of the picture books that were awarded the prestigious Caldecott Award over a fifteen-year period, Lenore Weitzman found that very few of the main characters presented were female.[28] When female characters were presented, they were primarily observers and were not central to the action. If adult females were presented, they were almost always shown wearing an apron. These books depicted a

primarily nurturant, helping, watching, domestic role for
females, even when the females were animals, such as Peter
Rabbit's mother. Weitzman also found that for every three titles
with female names, there were eight with male names, and for
each picture of a female, there were ten of males. These
educational materials reflect the overall values of our society.
They reinforce the high status of males and the low status of
females. And they do it in a humorous, affectionate way that is
hard to resist or even question when one is young.

Although most forces affecting young children continue to
reinforce traditional sex roles, many people are working
today to present non-sex-stereotypical environments to
children. Phyllis Taube Greenleaf reports on a group of teachers
in day-care centers and nursery schools who have been
attempting to learn how to counter some of the limiting aspects
of sex-role training. She describes the process as requiring
analysis and understanding of the problem, but as yielding
important results. The teachers have found that ignoring sex
roles is not sufficient to change the degree of sex-typicality in
children. By age three or four, many boys and girls sex-segregate
themselves and play more sex-typical games and activities.
Because of the heavy and consistent pressure on children to be
sex-typical, countering that effect requires a positive and active
approach. The teachers began to intervene in the sex-role-
stereotyping process by trying to understand the ways in which
they, as adults, consciously and unconsciously contributed to
sex-typing children. Thus, they had to confront their own
stereotypes and their own practices. They also had to challenge
sex-typical behavior of children. For example, they intervened
when children would say things such as "No, Larry, you can't
play here—boys don't cook," or "Girls don't play with cars!" The
teachers learned to step in and counter stereotypes by using
examples from the world around them. Teachers worked with
parents to show them that their children's non-sex-typical
interests—such as doll play for boys and vigorous athletics for
girls—were healthy and acceptable. They encouraged overly
docile girls to stand up for their rights, even if it meant
hitting back in certain circumstances.[29]

Sex-Role Identification

Although several sex-role socialization theorists disagree on exactly how and why it happens, all theorists agree that by age five or six, the average child has achieved strong identification with her or his own sex. Some theorists believe that children develop sex-role identification after conceptualizing the sex category and trying to fit their social behavior to it (cognitive-developmental theory).[30] Others assert that sex-role identification results from rewarding sex-appropriate behavior, punishing sex-inappropriate behavior, and offering loving models of the child's same sex for the child to imitate (social-learning theory).[31] Still other theorists believe that sex-role identification comes through a great emotional attachment to, and a desire to be like, the same-sex parent, which causes the child to incorporate the values and characteristics of that parent (psychoanalytic theory).[32] By the time children enter elementary school, they most likely think of themselves as members of their own sex, behave in sex-typical ways, want to be like members of their own sex, and feel emotionally committed to this point of view.

THREE:
Childhood

Getting the Message

BY THE TIME a child is five or six, she or he is intellectually
capable of viewing several aspects of a problem or object at once.
The six-year-old can understand some symbolization and can

accumulate a great deal of information.[1] Children now want to master information and comprehend the ways of society. During the childhood years—roughly from age six to age twelve—children want to know football players' names, RBI's (Runs Batted In), the capitals of the fifty states, solutions to math problems, when the first European came to the New World. The elementary-school-age child desires to be intellectually competent in a world that highly values such competence. Erik Erikson asserts that this stage of development poses the question to the child: "Are you industrious, or are you inferior?"[2] Now children want to achieve in the broader society beyond the family.

Whether they do in fact succeed will depend upon a number of factors, including the expectations of and support from significant people around them. This is also a period in which children are developing a clearer picture of themselves. The development of a positive self-image is crucial at this stage. Success in school and the approval of peers are both important to this self-image. While parents and the media continue to influence a child's development during this period, school and peers become increasingly significant.

Parents' Influence

As described earlier, mothers and fathers usually increase their sex-stereotyped demands and expectations as their children get older. By now, with help from TV and friends, the child is frequently a willing accomplice in the parents' stepped-up desires for a sex-typical child. At this stage, boys often play ball in the street daily, away from parental supervision. Girls play with dolls, arts and crafts projects, and board games, most often at home or in front of their own houses. They are usually more closely supervised by their parents, than are boys of the same age. Parents sometimes warn their young daughters not to play outside, especially by themselves, for fear of molestation by strange males. This may cause deep fears in girls and may contribute to their home-oriented play.[3]

Some children resist the pressure to conform to expected sex roles. Traditional parents may worry about the "normality" of these children and may devise various schemes, including psychotherapy, and material rewards for "appropriate" behavior, to gain conformity. Still some children refuse to conform, though often they suffer guilt and a sense of inadequacy in the process.

During the childhood years many parents, especially fathers, insist that their sons develop high levels of interest and skill in sports. In our society, a male athlete is considered highly masculine, and team sports (particularly aggressive contact sports) are seen by many as the height of male social groupings.

Marc Feigen Fasteau reports on interviews with men whose fathers had emphasized sports participation:

The father who pushes his son into sports with missionary zeal is so common as to be a part of our folklore. One man in his twenties, who described himself as having struck out more than any other nine-year-old on his Little League team, told me that his father literally carried him screaming and yelling to the games, where his relatives from a neighboring state across the river would sit in the stands to watch him play. And when he did poorly, his father wouldn't talk to him for several hours after the game. The fact that these extreme instances are funny, as well as sad, does not mean that the more usual climate is benign.[4]

Because boys are more likely to explore the outside world, use their bodies vigorously, engage in scientific games and mechanically oriented play, they develop different skills and interests than do girls, who engage in socially oriented activities such as dolls, dancing, board games, and reading. Intellectually these differences may lead to greater familiarity with what are called spatial-relations skills (mathematics, geometry, mechanics) in boys and social and verbal skills (reading, comprehension, and empathy) in girls.[5]

While most parents, regardless of social class background, raise their children in general accordance with sex-role standards, there are some differences between working-class and middle-class parents' adherence to them. A number of researchers have found that working-class parents tend to make earlier and more rigid sex-role distinctions in rearing their children compared to middle-class parents. For example, middle-class boys are more often permitted to express their emotions (including crying) and less often expected to be "tough" or "act like a man" in childhood than are working-class boys. A number of researchers attribute this class difference to parents' differing work experiences which can lead to different expectations for their children's future work and social roles.[6] Working-class parents may correctly perceive that their children have fewer work options and therefore must adhere strictly to whatever is considered the "norm." Middle-class children have more choices and will probably not be as severely "penalized" in the job market for being "different." Probably due to a complex combination of factors, working-class children are more aware of sex roles and subscribe earlier and more rigorously to them in their attitudes, choices of activities, and behaviors.[7]

Despite these generalizations about class differences, it is important to keep in mind the influence of ethnic diversity. Because working-class people are more likely to be closer to their ethnic roots than middle-class people, this diversity is more pronounced in the working class. It means that in some working-class families, displays of physical affection, crying, and other expressions of emotion are more acceptable for males than they are in some middle-class families. And within certain ethnic groups, women are more likely to take on family and religious leadership roles.

In some families in the United States, parents actively attempt to minimize sex-role stereotypes. These parents encourage their children to develop their interests and abilities regardless of what is considered "appropriate" for their sex. Many of these parents try to present themselves as nontypical sex-role models. A father may do a great deal of child care; he may become a good cook and housekeeper; he may try to explore his own emotional life and respond affectionately and emotionally to his children. A mother may work outside the home at a job she values. Her income may be necessary to support the family, and she may not take primary responsibility for the home and children. The parent(s) may self-consciously try to avoid presenting women as the guardians of the family's emotional and physical health and comfort and men as the breadwinners and decision makers. Parents who try to socialize their children to be non-sex-typical have to continuously battle their own past sex-role socialization, which often is deeply ingrained. They also have to withstand the influence and criticism of many other socialization agents with whom they come in contact: grandparents, teachers, neighbors. Having friends who share their values helps support parents who want to raise their children in non-sex-typical ways. In addition, parents who have jobs which permit flexibility, as well as the financial resources to pay for high-quality child care and frequent family vacations, may find it easier to present alternative models to their children.

Young Friends

A school playground offers a striking illustration of sex-role socialization: even among first-graders, children will probably be playing in small, unorganized, sex-segregated groups. Children of this age play primarily with friends of their own sex. Generally this is of their own choice—but not necessarily of their own *free* choice. These children are simply reflecting, in their behavior and attitudes, what they think is expected or required of them. They have come to understand the sex category and, further, they have come to accept and internalize it. They now believe in it as a way of life. Between six and twelve years of age, children will often resist attempts to mix the sexes in games or in other social situations. This is the age where sex-segregated birthday parties, boys' Little League, girls' jump rope games, Brownie and Cub Scouts are common experiences for children.

In one study on sex differences, fifth-grade children were asked to perform in a word game. One of the experimental conditions required competing against a same-sex child. When the children were asked to change their seats so they would be sitting next to a child of their own sex, the boys in the class began to shout and refused to "give up" their chairs to girls or sit in girls' chairs. The boys claimed the girls had "cooties." Interestingly, the girls in the class did not seem to mind switching chairs with the boys, but giggled in an approving manner when the boys shouted "cooties."[8] Sex-segregation patterns in childhood may seem quite silly, but they are very real.

Most boys spend large amounts of time playing football, baseball, soccer, stickball, or hockey. Sports serve as the major social arena for school-age boys. The boys who play ball together often become very good friends, largely because they share this activity. Boys who play on the same Little League team or play stickball together on the block often function as a tight-knit boys club. The rough-and-tumble style of many boys puts great pressure on boys who are not so sex-typical. For the less athletic, less aggressive, or more studious boys, the peer group can present a great threat. Epithets of "sissy," "faggot," or "goody-goody" can be very painful tools to force boys to comply with sex-role standards insisted upon by the peer group. When children respond to each other in such a cruel fashion, it is probably due to their own insecurity about sex roles. A boy of eight or ten is a relatively new convert to sex roles. He still views them rigidly and is often afraid to break what he perceives to be hard-and-fast rules of behavior. When he sees another boy "breaking" these rules, it may raise questions of his own sex-role definition. Often, the child who takes the offensive against another child's non-sex-typical behavior is really trying to cover up his own insecurities about sex roles.

While much research has shown that boys refuse to play with girls or with "typically feminine" toys and activities, girls are somewhat less likely to reject boys and their games.[9] This is not to say that girls are usually eager to play with boys or "masculine" toys. But girls, along with boys, learn that males, and things related to males, have high status and value and are often associated with personal freedom in our society. So girls usually feel more ambivalent.[10] On the one hand, the girl wants to be "feminine" because that is her sex category and is thus socially appropriate for her. On the other hand, she wants to be—and have things that are—highly valued in our society. Studies that ask girls and boys which games and toys they would prefer to play with show that girls more often than boys say they would prefer activities associated with the opposite sex. Girls usually prefer to play more often with boys than vice versa. And girls more often say they would prefer to be boys than boys say they would prefer to be girls. Karen Horney calls this status envy: females may realize their inferior position or status in society and may thus wish to switch places with the more valued sex.[11] This may be why "tomboyism" is quite common among elementary-school-age girls.

What is most interesting is that other girls, adults, and even boys do not seem to mind this semireversed behavior in girls as much as they mind it in boys. This is due to many factors. Probably most importantly, our culture harbors the belief that males are superior to females (false as that idea may be), and so if a girl wishes to act like a boy it is understandable. "But why would a male choose to act like a devalued female?" a sophisticated child or a parent might wonder. Since people have more trouble understanding why boys behave in non-sex-typical ways than why girls do, parents and others may be particularly concerned about non-sex-typical behavior in males. They may believe that a male who acts in traditionally "feminine" ways is latently homosexual. Another reason why people may interpret a male child's "feminine" behavior as homosexual more than they interpret a female child's "masculine" behavior in that way is that males in our culture are frequently, though falsely, seen as more sexual. Fear of homosexuality and of other non-traditional sex-role behavior is common in our culture partly because we rely on traditional sex roles to define and structure so much of our social lives.

Elementary School

Researchers have found that children and adults perceive the formal elementary school environment as feminine. In some studies, elementary school children describe school objects such as books and chalkboards as feminine.[12] And when children were asked what their teachers wanted from them, the children emphasized good behavior over good academic work. [13] The characteristics that the schools reward—obedience, passivity, and quietness—are stereotypically feminine. In addition, with 85 percent of all elementary school teachers being female and 78 percent of the administrators (principals and assistant principals) male, the traditional home setting and power structure is replicated in schools.[14]

Children have the impression that school and its requirements are feminine and they have already learned that females
and femininity are generally devalued in our society. Boys, in
order to maintain a sense of masculinity, may feel compelled to
reject school or defy the behavior that most schools require of
them. Not incidentally, these requirements are most often
articulated by the teachers, who are generally female. On the
other hand, girls, in attempting to increase their sense of
femininity, may further internalize and act out those characteristics most valued in many schools. This often means quiet
docility and obedience to authority. Neither total acceptance
nor total rejection of school values is very healthy for the
developing individual. For the many boys who reject their
teachers' demands, academic failure is a good possibility. If the
male peer group is waiting in the back of the classroom to cheer
on defiance and to smirk at cooperation and achievement, the
learning process becomes less attractive to boys. As a result, boys
are found to have more learning problems, lower grades, and
more behavior problems than girls in elementary schools.[15] This
negative attitude toward school means that many young boys do
not learn basic skills. This may limit later opportunities for
personal, intellectual, and academic growth.

Girls are harmed by this sex-role dichotomy in school in a very
different way. Although girls tend to do well in school and to
enjoy the experience, their early performance may establish
learning patterns that can limit future achievement and self-
growth. As children grow older, increasingly achievement
involves risk taking, exploration, independent thinking, self-
confidence, and an active approach to problem solving. The
passive learning patterns girls master in childhood make later
achievement more difficult.[16]

Many teachers both expect and reward sex-typical behavior
patterns in children. In one study, a sample group of fifth- and
sixth-grade teachers encouraged independence and autonomy in
boys they perceived as bright while encouraging dependence and
"good work habits" in average boys and in bright and average
girls.[17] Other studies indicate that teachers offered more
approval and disapproval to boys than to girls, and that boys

received more feedback from and had more interaction with their teachers than did girls.[18] When teachers expressed disapproval, they disciplined boys for not following the rules, for being sloppy, or for lack of effort; they more often disciplined girls for lack of knowledge or ability.[19] While the boy who doesn't "follow the rules" may receive disapproval from his teacher, he generally gets support from his peer group in class. The girl being disapproved of by her teacher finds no solace from her friends and may see the matter as a personal failing.

One school system, believing strongly in differences between the sexes, decided to sex-segregate their elementary school classes. An administrator describes some teaching methods that were used in the sex-segregated classes:

1. In working with boys, we employ more science materials and experiments. There is more emphasis on building things and on studies of transportation. As a result, we can create and maintain a high level of interest.

2. We have found it well to let the interests of the classes guide the teacher in areas such as science and social studies. Depending on the sex of the group, this sometimes results in quite different activities. From studying the atom, for example, a boy's class moved easily into a study of nuclear fission. It is unlikely that girls would respond in this way. Or another example, mold can be studied from a medical standpoint by boys and in terms of cooking by girls.

3. In all-boy and all-girl classes, we have used different songs and rhythms. For girls we use quieter games, fairy stories, and games and songs which emphasize activities such as sewing and housekeeping. For boys, we use more active physical games which involve noise and muscle movement and are based on a transportation theme.

4. Different reading stories are also used. Girls enjoy all stories in readers, even those about boys, but boys do not like stories about girls. Boys prefer tales and stories about industry, transportation and vocations. The same differentiation applies to creative writing.[20]

This school system is clear about sex-typing children. More commonly, schools sex-type students in subtle ways, but the message is essentially the same.

Most school systems share the dominant values of our society. They are training children to fit in to conventional roles. Now, however, many people realize how harmful heavy sex-role socialization can be, especially in light of the changing roles of women and men. Some teachers are aware of the problems and limit their sex-role socializing of students. But many of those who have valiantly tried to make changes have met some serious obstacles: school administrators who may subscribe to traditional sex-role values; parents who fear their children will not grow up to be "normal." In addition, most TV shows and movies tell children what "real boys" and "real girls" are like and teach them to be fearful of trying non-sex-typical activities. The classroom teacher can make some important changes, but she or he needs help from the broader community as well.

A review of educational materials illustrates how sex roles are solidified and legitimated for children. In readers used in most elementary schools, just as in picture books described earlier, the vast majority of stories are about males. The few stories about females tend to describe the female's main function as helping someone else. In one children's reader, seven out of eight stories are about males and the one story with a female main character is brief—ten pages compared to forty to sixty pages for other stories in the book. The girl in the tale is primarily described as assisting her mother, and her brother who goes hunting.[21] In a review of elementary school textbooks, a group of researchers found that stories which involved ingenuity, cleverness, creativity, industry, strength, bravery, autonomy, and assertiveness were almost always about males. Stories involving friendship, repetitive tasks, helpfulness, and emotionality were usually about females. These same researchers found an appalling lack of biographies of females, which helps give the elementary school child the impression that history was devoid of women.[22]

In an analysis of pictures and problems used in math textbooks, Marsha Federbush finds a similar situation: boys are active and good at math, girls mainly sit around feeling bewildered about the problems.[23] In one such math book a boy actually states, "I guess girls are no good in math." Federbush

girls are limited in what they can do occupationally.

describes the presentation of mathematical sets which she calls "sets by sex": males doing "typical male" things are grouped in one set and females doing "typical female" things are grouped in another set. She quotes a first-grade girl who tells her mother, "I can't be a doctor, only a nurse. My [math] book says so." The first-grader made this comment after studying mathematical sets containing large numbers of male doctors and female nurses. Instructional materials tell children that history, adventure, and high achievement are for boys while nurturance, home, friendship, and mothering are for girls. Children get the message.

Marcia Guttentag, an educational psychologist, decided to test whether a school's conscious effort at altering children's attitudes toward sex roles could make a significant difference.[24] She set up experimental intervention programs in three public school districts in the Boston area. The program involved teachers and their students in kindergarten, fifth, and ninth grades. The teachers were trained to fulfill the goals of the program, and special curriculum materials and activities were provided to aide their efforts. The teachers were instructed to encourage all students to participate in play activities and interact with one another in non-sex-typical ways. They tried to help students imagine themselves in many different kinds of adult roles. The two older groups were helped to develop some awareness of the sex-role stereotyping that exists in literature, the media, and occupational roles. In addition, the program was designed to help the oldest group of students think critically about the limiting aspects of traditional sex-role stereotyping.

Participating students' attitudes toward sex roles were measured before and after the intervention program to gauge change. After four to six weeks, some changes were apparent. The youngest group experienced the most change from the intervention program. The oldest group changed the least; in fact, some ninth-grade boys seemed quite hostile and expressed even more extreme traditional sex-role attitudes after the intervention program. Generally, girls were more open to the changes encouraged by the program than were boys. Defensiveness on the part of the boys seemed apparent at the two older age levels. Perhaps the boys perceived they were being challenged both in their superior position and their power. Possibly too much emphasis was placed on females to the exclusion of males and the boys may thus have felt left out or threatened. It was also suggested that the ninth-grade teachers were not as enthusiastic about the program as were the lower-grade teachers; this was at least partially due to logistical problems in administering the program. However, one ninth-grade teacher expressed a high degree of interest in and commitment to the program. That teacher's male as well as female students became more positive about alternative sex roles. A number of conclusions can be drawn from this intervention program: first, children's attitudes toward sex roles can be changed; second, changing sex-role attitudes may be easier with young children; and third, a teacher with a positive attitude and commitment to sex-role alternatives will be most able to affect change with any age group.

Parents can also influence the schools' policy on and awareness of traditional sex roles. At Woodward School, a private elementary school in Brooklyn, New York, a group of parents formed a sex-roles committee in order to help teachers and administrators become aware of their own sex-role attitudes and behavior and also to provide them with curriculum materials to help them effect change in the children. At first the parents' committee and the school staff were at odds. But after much time and effort, they were able to work together to offer the children an educational environment that did not limit them by rigid sex-role stereotypes. The principal of the school commented: "I think that even the most resistant staff member has moved. I think even if people are not ready to *be* different, they're ready to *act* differently. I think they now see many instances of sexism where they didn't see it before." A number of the teachers said that they strongly encouraged boys to express their emotions and girls to develop their strength and competence, especially in gym, math, and shop. One teacher criticized herself for being too strident, initially, in her desire to teach non-sex-typical behavior: "I bludgeoned and came on too strong and turned the kids off." With time, experience, and support from other teachers and parents, she learned to weave alternatives to traditional sex roles more naturally into the curriculum. Her growing awareness of the pervasiveness of sex roles helped her to find ways to teach about alternatives while minimizing fear and defensiveness on the part of the students.[25]

The presence of groups of parents, teachers, and students interested in creating a nonsexist curriculum has forced some major textbook publishing companies to revise the language (not always using "he" when meaning male or female) and, more rarely, the content of the textbooks. Although the changes have often been superficial, new textbooks are, on the whole, somewhat less sexist than they have been in the past.

Achievement Motivation

There is nothing inherently wrong with a child having some or even many sex-typical characteristics, with being feminine or being masculine. The problem lies in the extremity of the two stereotypes and the limits each extreme imposes on the development of the individual. Research has shown that most girls will work hard to achieve if social approval is available, whereas they are less likely to strive for success when immediate approval from others is not available.[26] Males, even in the elementary school years, tend to be more likely to strive for success at a task because of their desire for accomplishment. From very early in a female's life, she is encouraged to achieve, but to achieve in an obedient, conforming, dependent , and other-oriented fashion. Her creativity is often ignored and her mistakes are magnified. Most girls have few role models of females who are highly successful, and so assume that members of their sex can be good, but not special, not great, and not very smart.

While girls get better grades than boys through high school and on into college, their expectations for future success are significantly lower. Girls are not underachievers in school; quite the contrary. Girls' performance is most often stable and good, especially compared to boys'. But girls do not think of themselves as so good and often shrink from real challenges and competition. Girls tend to underestimate how capable they are and to believe they will do poorly. This low expectation makes them more anxious about their performance and less confident about fulfilling a difficult task. So girls often give up, even though they may have the necessary skills to achieve. In one study, girls and boys were asked to do a series of academic tasks. They were told which tasks they did correctly and which ones they did incorrectly. Then the children were asked to choose a task they would like to repeat. Most of the boys chose to repeat the tasks they did not do correctly the first time, while most of the girls chose the tasks they already knew how to do.[27] Challenges and risks must be taken in order to reap real returns. But since challenge is taught as "masculine," girls often shrink from it, preferring instead to stay with the low-risk and low-gain mode of achievement. This characteristically "feminine" behavior will make it harder for girls to forge their ways into new fields, new jobs, new social roles.

Boys, on the other hand, are trained to be somewhat defiant and independent. Middle-class boys in particular are not expected to get approval for obedience, but rather for their special creativity and skills, or even for their rebellion. Successful male role models are plentiful, especially for middle-class boys, and everyone expects the male ultimately to achieve in some line of work or study. But what about those boys who do not pay attention in class, partly to fulfill the male sex-role stereotype? What about the boys who define masculine as "muscles" and feminine as "bookwormish"? Their lack of skills may hurt them in later achievement. These males often have low self-expectations; since they do not expect to achieve very much, they do not expend the effort necessary to do so. In fact, for many boys from poor or working-class families, this may be a somewhat realistic response to the opportunities available to them. A vast number of jobs do not require a great deal of creativity or analytical thinking. These skills can even be a detriment in certain jobs where passivity and obeying orders are most highly valued. The problem is that most jobs in the contemporary United States do require some level of literacy. If boys reject school too thoroughly, they will not be able to fulfill this basic requirement.

Many of the most prestigious and high-paying jobs in our society are reserved for the analytic thinker with enough self-control for consistent hard work. One theorist asserts that those most likely to achieve success are neither extremely passive, conforming, and inhibited children (most typically girls) nor extremely bold and impulsive children (most typically boys). Rather, an individual who is moderate in both dimensions is more likely to be sufficiently independent and self-disciplined to pursue an idea and master it. This style of learning is neither typically feminine nor typically masculine but combines aspects of both categories.

FOUR:
Adolescence

Between Childhood and Adulthood

ADOLESCENCE OFFICIALLY BEGINS with the onset of puberty and ends in the late teens or early twenties. It is the bridge between childhood and adulthood. However, the child does not instantly

46

become an adolescent with biological-sexual maturity. Between the ages of ten and thirteen, youngsters find themselves caught in between, being treated as children (and partly wanting to be) and seeing the next step ahead: independence, increased sexuality, and being grownup. Excessive giggling, concern with nudity, and alternating of mature behavior with downright silliness marks the preadolescent or prepubertal child. People warn the preadolescent not to grow up too fast. Yet the models for adolescence and adulthood call out via the older teenagers in the neighborhood, TV, movie stars, makeup commercials, teen and romance magazines. Adolescence is usually an extremely

exciting period because the individual has begun to act on her or his own behalf, to consciously make her or his own decisions. The sense of strength is exhilarating. But the teenager often confronts dangers and uncertainties that can also make this period of development frightening.

One of the major goals of adolescence is the clearer development of a full sense of personal identity: determining who one is, in one's own eyes and in the eyes of others, and who one wants to be. Throughout life, people shape and alter their identities . But during adolescence, this process is particularly intense, involving, and important, because of many dramatic changes in the nature of relationships with friends and family and because of new demands and expectations.

Sex roles are particularly important to adolescents, partly because biological sex differences become much more pronounced at this time. One's sex and sexuality may dominate one's sense of self. Physical changes are signs to the self and to others that the developing individual will soon be an adult; the rush is on to prepare or socialize the adolescent for her or his future adult sex role.

Biological Changes

For girls, signs of sexual maturity generally appear between the ages of eleven and fourteen, although they often appear earlier or later than that. Menstruation begins, ovaries and uterus increase in size and become capable of carrying a fetus. Breasts develop, pubic and underarm hair appear, hips fill out, and a general growth spurt occurs. For boys, puberty usually comes a couple of years later, between thirteen and sixteen years of age, though as with girls, the age of onset varies greatly. With puberty, the penis and testicles increase in size and young men develop the ability to ejaculate (release semen containing sperm cells upon sexual climax or orgasm). Body, facial, pubic, and underarm hair appear, the voice deepens, and a large growth spurt occurs. Puberty in both males and females is caused by a change in the regulation of hormones by part of the brain called the hypothalmus. This change causes the ovaries of the female to produce more estrogen and the testes of the male to produce more testosterone. These changes in hormones stimulate the physical and sexual development of individuals.

There are several important differences in the nature of puberty for males and females. First, females experience the onset of menstruation in a fairly sudden fashion. At once a girl knows something has changed her into a young woman. This usually becomes family knowledge. For the boy, puberty is a more gradual process. While a boy may awake one morning to realize that he has ejaculated during his sleep, the finding is usually private and does not automatically bring forth information on hygiene or acknowledgment from the family. Second, female puberty comes earlier than male puberty, usually by about two years. Young women, who often are encouraged to be modest, may find it hard to accept their obviously developing bodies. Especially for early developing females, there may be considerable embarrassment about budding breasts, increased height, and being one of the first in the class or crowd to menstruate. Puberty brings a new interest in sexuality. Since girls experience puberty before boys do, they may be more socially and sexually advanced than their male peers. Studies have found that early-maturing girls are self-conscious and see themselves as awkward and embarrassed, while early-maturing boys have good self-images and see themselves as popular and athletic.[1] The early-maturing boys get to be the first to respond to the girls' advances and are seen as special. It is also possible that womanhood is less attractive to the girl than manhood is to the boy.

A further difference between the impact of puberty on males and females is related to the biology of and social demands surrounding pregnancy. Puberty to females means, among other things, the ability to become pregnant and therefore the possibility of becoming a mother. This is a mixed blessing to the young woman who, not yet an adult herself, is beginning to explore her own sexuality. Adolescents may be especially fearful of pregnancy, since many parents do not introduce their daughters to birth control when menstruation and possible sexual activity begin. While more and more people expect similar behavior from females and males, many people still believe that a "nice girl" should not be interested in sex and should not engage in sexual activity, either by herself (masturbation) or with another person. There are many more taboos against the expression of female sexuality than of male sexuality. If anything, males may be pushed into sexual activity before they are really interested. But the pubescent female may find herself fearing sexual contact because of damage to her social reputation or fear of pregnancy. Fear of pregnancy is a theme that recurs throughout women's sexual lives until they cease to menstruate in middle adulthood (usually around age forty-eight to fifty-five).

Beauty and "Sexploitation"

In Western society, a great deal of emphasis is placed on female beauty. From infancy on, female physical "attractiveness" is stressed by family, friends, TV, movies, magazines. During adolescence, feminine beauty becomes central: most young women spend a great deal of time fussing over clothes, makeup, and "slimnastics." The "pretty" young women may be the most popular during adolescence. With so much emphasis on external appearance and approval from others, the average female teenager is not encouraged to develop intellectual skills or qualities such as independence and the ability to work in groups. She is less likely than males her age to develop a strong sense of who she is and what she is capable of doing with her life. Many especially beautiful women, including adolescents, fear that people care for them only because of their looks. They worry that their personalities and their minds are ignored by others. As her appearance changes over the years and no longer fits the strict standards our society holds, the female who is obsessed with her looks may have a particularly difficult time.

"Attractiveness" is also important for adolescent males, but in different ways. Size, strength, and athletic prowess are considered highly desirable in young men. But with age, achievement— especially in holding a stable, well-paying job— is an important aspect of a male's appeal. "You can love a rich man as easily as a poor man" is a common piece of advice for young women. The focus on achievement, in sports early on and in employment later, puts a great deal of pressure on males to be competitive. As adolescents look toward adulthood, they feel the pressure to be either a beautiful woman or an achieving man: each is a stereotype that may exclude important aspects of the individual's development.

"Beauty" can be seen as a set of characteristics that are specified by a particular culture. The standards of what is "beautiful" are different in different cultures. Standards of beauty shift even within a culture. The American bathing beauties of the 1930s would be considered a bit chubby by today's standards of extreme slenderness. Definitions of beauty are popularized and communicated through the most effective media available within a culture. In a primitive society, this would probably happen via face-to-face verbal communication and artistic works. The process of change would be slow and the uniformity would not be so great. In Western culture, TV, movies, and magazines set the trends for fashion and the standards for beauty. Change is rapid and the message is conveyed clearly to all of us.

In the United States and much of the industrialized world, television is perhaps the best communicator of cultural values of beauty. While many "beautiful" people (especially women) are displayed on TV shows, commercials provide the most vivid lessons on beauty and its great importance for females. Here beauty is used to sell products. Viewers are told that women must be sexy, skinny, elaborately made up, and elegantly dressed. They should also smell like flowers, have hairless armpits and legs, wear stylish hairdos, and be natural! While many women, young and old, rich and poor, black and white, are checking to make sure they get as close to fulfilling these images as possible, primarily through buying many products, the advertisers and manufacturers are making large profits. The beauty and fashion industries rely on women's insecurities about how they look to sell their products. Market researchers are employed to find out the best ways to appeal to women's desire to be beautiful. The social outcome of advertising is to reinforce emphasis on female beauty and females' insecurities about their own attractiveness.

The issue of hair is a good case in point. Females often think their hair is too straight, too curly, too thin, too thick, or the wrong color. The point is that so many females see themselves as inadequately attractive. Certainly this makes females as a group a wonderful market for beauty aids and the latest fashions—all to make up for their perceived basic unattractiveness.

It is important to note that standard definitions of female beauty are focused on the white, middle-class woman. William Grier and Price Cobb describe the difficulty that many black females experience in developing positive images of how they look. They suggest that many black females judge themselves by white standards—being blond, blue-eyed, fine featured—and feel themselves to be quite unattractive.[2] Other researchers assert that, more recently, black women have been turning toward other black women as role models of beauty and are judging themselves more positively.[3] However, this new black standard for beauty is still highly influenced by the black models chosen to sell products. Women of all races are caught in the bind of being exposed to, and most often accepting, commercialized standards of attractiveness for all women.

One hazardous manifestation of the ethic of female beauty is anorexia nervosa, a disease that consists of excessive weight loss: commonly one third of the person's total body weight. The syndrome includes self-imposed starvation, as well as binging on food and then purging one's system by vomiting or using laxatives. It often requires hospitalization and has caused many deaths. Although instances of anorexia nervosa occur among some males and have been known to occur in other cultures, the disease appears in epidemic proportions among adolescent females in the contemporary United States. Most people who have such excessive weight loss believe they are "fat" regardless of their weight. Adolescent women with this syndrome were frequently considered by others to be extremely attractive before their weight loss. Yet these young women usually felt they were not attractive enough.[4] For victims of anorexia nervosa, striving to meet a culturally defined standard of beauty—slimness—can be life-threatening.

Some of the same messages that teach women to conform to certain standards of beauty, teach men to respond to women's sexual attractiveness with unbridled aggressiveness. The result is a high frequency of male sexual aggression and violence against females. Adolescent boys are told that "real men" get what they want sexually and that an attractive woman is "asking for it." This can translate into men sexually forcing themselves onto unwilling women they are close to, often hurting them, frightening them, and making them feel degraded. Gisela Konopka interviewed 920 teenage women and found that almost all females who reported having intercourse before age fourteen said they were raped by a male relative or "friend" of the family.[5] In addition, a significant number of men sexually attack women or girls who are total strangers to them. These rapes can be terribly damaging, especially when many people in our culture believe that rape is an understandable response to female sexual attractiveness and beauty. Often the female victim feels guilty and blames herself. A woman may be frightened to tell authorities, friends, or relatives about a rape, because she fears she will be treated as the criminal or instigator. One judge who presided over a case involving a rape victim was known to say of the rapist, "After all, he was just trying to show her a good time."[6] Other judges have permitted questions to be asked of the rape victim that pertain to her previous sexual experiences or her clothing and underwear at the time of the rape. These questions imply that a woman's attractiveness or sexuality could "cause" a rape, and that the rapist therefore should not be blamed for his attraction to her and his attack.[7] Recently laws have been passed that make it somewhat easier for women to report rapes to the police and to get psychological counseling and legal abortions if they need and want these services.[8] These changes, plus the newly available services for rape victims, go part of the way in convincing people that rape is the fault and crime of the rapist, not the victim. These changes have come about through the prolonged political efforts of feminist groups which have identified the practice of rape as a particularly oppressive crime against females of all social classes, of all ages, and of all racial and ethnic groups.

The female beauty/male aggressive response pattern is one damaging aspect of sex-role stereotypes. As more women reject the commercialized standards of beauty and rely on their health, cleanliness, strength, and personality to be attractive, and as more men alter their aggressive responses to females, more areas of personal growth and mutual respect will be open to females and males.

Teenage Sexuality

The majority of adolescents want to have close, meaningful relationships with individuals of the opposite sex. This is especially true for girls.[9] Most of these romantic relationships include sexual sharing of some kind, though this may mean kissing for some couples and intercourse for others. Exploring one's own and another's sexual responses and abilities is exciting and can be quite enjoyable. However, due to lack of sexual experience, the sexual aspects of adolescent relationships can be disappointing. It generally takes time, patience, and experience for people to learn about their own sexual needs in order for sex to be truly pleasurable. Since adolescents shift relationships relatively frequently, they rarely have the experience of learning about the sexual needs and styles of one partner. Feelings of self-doubt, insecurities about "going too far," and fear of pregnancy also create tensions in teenage relationships.

Males and females are usually socialized to view their participation in sex in different ways. While more and more people have come to reject the "double standard," many adolescents still learn that "good girls" don't engage in sexual intercourse until marriage, while "real boys" want sex with anyone they can find. The stereotype of dating behavior is that he wants "all he can get" without a commitment and she wants a commitment before she gives her all. The adolescent girl who is sexually assertive and wants to explore her sexuality may be defined as "fast" or "loose." The adolescent boy who wants to take his time and build a close emotional relationship before sharing an extended sexual relationship may be considered feminine or a goody-goody. Preconceived ideas of what males and females should be like limit individual choices and serve to make a significant number of people feel sexually and/or socially inadequate or abnormal. The double standard can create anxieties for individuals and can lead to a great deal of tension for the dating couple. Females may fear both the sexual act and the idea of being abandoned or rejected by the person with whom sex is shared. Many females feel guilty and unfeminine for expressing their sexuality. Young males may feel pressured to be sexually aggressive even if this is not their own personal inclination. And power games may be played so that the person with the greatest amount of power in the relationship gets to have his or her sexual way.[10]

While the double standard greatly influences the ways in which males and females feel about their sexuality, recent research indicates that it does not dramatically influence their behavior. Although there are contradictory findings on the extent of sexual intercourse among teenagers, the estimates are that from 21 to 33 percent of high school boys and from 19 to 55 percent of high school girls (depending on the year in school and the geographical location of the students) engage in sexual intercourse. For college students, the estimates are as high as 82 percent for males and 85 percent for females. What appears to be a higher percentage of females engaging in sexual intercourse at each age may be due, at least in part, to the common practice in American society of younger females dating somewhat older males. One statistic for all age groups indicates that 60 percent of all males and 40 percent of all females have had premarital intercourse. (Keep in mind that the average age of marriage is 21 for females and 22 for males.) Clearly females as well as males are engaging in sexual intercourse at a fairly high rate.[11] Although many adolescents happily choose to be sexually active, it is possible that new sexual norms put pressure on some females and males to engage in sexual activity whether or not they really want to.

Adolescent heterosexual (male-female) relationships are often, but not always, accompanied by extremely traditional sex-role behavior. Some heterosexual adolescents find traditional sex roles too rigid and confining, and so they alter the sex roles for their own use. More commonly, though, the adolescent male feels pressured to "act like a man" and so may become quite domineering and nonexpressive of his emotions outside of an explicitly sexual context. The female may feel that once she has a boyfriend, she has to assume all those feminine behaviors she has heard of, read about, and seen on TV and in real life. Young women often become extremely dependent on their boyfriends. Adolescent men and women are behaving in what they perceive to be "correct" ways: they are trying on adult sex roles.

Although many adolescents engage in sexual intercourse, masturbation (genital self-stimulation usually leading to orgasm) is the sexual act most frequently practiced by adolescents. Almost all males and about two-thirds of all females report masturbating.[12] Masturbation is more frequently practiced when an individual is not in a sexual relationship with another person. For males, masturbation is usually the first type of sexual experience; for females, masturbation most often occurs after orgasm has been experienced in a sexual encounter with another person. Recent research suggests that a large number of females experience orgasm exclusively via masturbation and that others experience their strongest and/or multiple orgasms during masturbation.[13]

Masturbation does not reach its peak for females until their twenties, while this practice tends to peak for males in their mid-teens. This sex difference in masturbation may be due in part to stereotypical values. It may take the average female until young adulthood to reject the idea that she is not supposed to be sexual.

In many families, masturbation is viewed very negatively. Young children may be punished for touching their genitals; adolescents may be warned that masturbation leads to insanity or poor eyesight. Even in families in which taboos against masturbation are not overtly discussed, the silence and secrecy surrounding masturbation can cause many adolescents to feel "deviant" or "sinful" about this common sexual practice. This is especially true for females, who rarely share information on this topic with anyone else. Because there are general taboos against females' exploration of and knowledge about their genitals, masturbation may appear to most young women to be unfeminine and mysterious. But just as the double standard has not prevented teenage women from participating in sex with partners, taboos against masturbation have not stopped young women from masturbating. Instead, the societal message contributes to females' feelings of guilt about their sexual experiences and adds, therefore, to their poor self-images.

Adolescents are independent in many ways, but they are still dependent on the "norms," the social definitions of what is correct and what is incorrect for people to do. One norm that is generally accepted by adults and adolescents is that of heterosexual coupling (a male and a female engaged in a personal-sexual relationship.) During adolescence, such relationships are reinforced while other kinds of sexual relationships are often criticized or even cruelly punished. Although the majority of people are heterosexual during adolescence and later adulthood, many other people are not. Most adolescents know of a few people in their classes, workplaces, or neighborhoods who defy the "norm" by being openly homosexual (personal-sexual relationships with a same-sex partner) or bisexual (personal-sexual relationships with either a same- or opposite-sex partner). Many homosexual and bisexual people do not overtly express their sexual preferences because they fear social, personal, and economic repercussions. Homosexuality and bisexuality have been and are widely practiced and accepted in various cultures. For example, in ancient Greek society, male homosexuality was considered the highest form of personal-sexual relationship. But our society has been marked by a great fear of nonheterosexuality. In some states there are laws prohibiting homosexuals from holding government jobs, including teaching. In addition, in all but a few cities, it is fully legal to discriminate against lesbians and gay men in housing, employment, and public accommodations. Many parents consider themselves failures if their sons or daughters have homosexual or bisexual preferences. Fear of homosexuality and bisexuality is not based on factual evidence; research has shown that most homosexuals and bisexuals live relatively healthy, happy, and productive lives.[14]

The social, economic, and political harassment directed

against homosexuals and bisexuals can make their lives difficult. During adolescence, this harassment is particularly strong because young people, in a search for their own sexual identities, often feel threatened by the presence of alternatives to heterosexuality. Choices may appear confusing and fear-provoking to the adolescent who is anxious about success in the heterosexual world. The presence of homosexuals and bisexuals raises questions: "Could I be gay too?" "If homosexuality isn't sick, then how do I know if I'm healthy?" "How can I choose a sexual life-style that I enjoy?" "Do I have a choice?"

A substantial percentage of males (37 percent) and females (13 percent) engage in some form of homosexual behavior during adolescence.[15] For the majority of teenagers, homosexual encounters are short-lived and may not indicate commitment to a homosexual preference. They are part of a general exploration of one's sexuality. For some, an early homosexual encounter marks a clear sexual preference; in these cases, it is often met with pleasure and relief.[16]

Most lesbians and gay men experience their first homosexual attractions and/or sexual relationships when they are teenagers. Their awareness of themselves as gays often grows during adolescence.[17] Since this is a period in which the dominating peer group strongly and openly supports traditional heterosexuality, adolescence can be a difficult period for individuals with homosexual preferences. In the past, few models have been publicly available to help young gays in developing their homosexual identity.[18] Gay men and lesbians have often experienced conflict and fears as adolescents because they have not known many other gay people and have had little accurate information on gay life-styles.[19] Many have feared rejection by their parents or other family members. In some cases, adolescent homosexuals have been put into psychiatric hospitals or forced into intensive therapy in an attempt to change their sexual preferences.[20]

Several studies indicate that the majority of lesbians and male gays "came out" as homosexuals (that is, began to develop a clear homosexual identity and public social status) once they found others to support them through a period of transition. Often this occurred in such all-male or all-female environments as the armed services, same-sex colleges, or specifically gay meeting places such as bars.

Lesbians, according to many studies, are more likely than heterosexual women to question and reject the traditional female social roles, thus rejecting the restrictions placed on women in our society.[21] As children, they were more likely to engage in nontraditionally feminine behaviors which were often labeled by others as tomboyism.[22] The reasons for this, however, are quite complex. In a compilation of autobiographical accounts by lesbians, a number of writers indicated that as adolescents growing up prior to the 1970s and the influence of the gay liberation movement, they thought that the only choice they had was to be "masculine."[23] The only models of relationships available to them involved behaving according to traditional sex role models. Studies of male homosexuals indicate a similar pattern in which an individual was typecast as feminine because he had some "nonmasculine" interests or else felt compelled to behave in a feminine fashion since, allegedly, that was male homosexual behavior.[24] With greater public acceptance and knowledge of homosexuality, and with a larger number of gay people publicly "out" as homosexuals, many adolescents and adults are more aware of the complexities of sex roles and sexuality. Consequently, fewer lesbians may feel trapped into playing the male role and fewer male gays may feel compelled to be stereotypically feminine.

The emergence of the gay rights movement ten years ago has resulted in a growing number of support groups of and for lesbians and gay males. For example, there are gay clubs in many colleges as well as gay religious groups of Catholics, Protestants, and Jews. The first National Third World Lesbian and Male Gay Conference was held in 1979. It brought together blacks, Hispanics, Asian Americans, and Native Americans to discuss their mutual and distinct problems and solutions. Support groups offer gays, especially teenagers, people to turn to to share their experiences of emerging homosexuality. This can minimize the isolation that teenagers contemplating a homosexual preference may experience.

Family Relationships

During adolescence, independence and the pleasure of mastering new skills are very important. Adult roles are tried on without the full responsibilities that eventually will be attached to them. In the United States the future roles of men and women are not as clearly defined as they are in some other societies. Margaret Mead studied adolescents in Samoa, an island in the South Seas.[25] She found that there, adolescence was marked by a smooth transition to adulthood: adolescents had clear responsibilities and were unambivalent about their future roles, including their sex roles. Partly, they were not aware of, and thus not terribly interested in, other alternatives. For adolescents in the United States, the transition is often difficult. Because of the many social, political, and economic changes taking place, confusing and tantalizing options appear to exist. For example, while adolescents are aware of the traditional sex-role definitions in the society and are strongly influenced by them, they are also conscious of alternatives. Young women today often perceive that they may have a career, be involved in politics, or participate in sports. Some women realize that having or not having children can be a personal choice. Young women and men may see that they can choose the type of personal-sexual relationship they will be involved in. For young men, working slavishly to maintain a dependent family may no longer be the only model for adulthood. Some men consider the option of sharing in child care and domestic tasks, exploring closer friendships with others, and developing many interests outside of their work lives.

When adolescents try out new ideas, new ways to live and grow, parents, teachers, other adults, and even friends may label the behavior as "rebellion." Trying out new roles and alternatives is often genuine and is not necessarily meant to hurt or anger other people. But parents and others may not be pleased to see the young person rejecting their more traditional values. In addition, many adolescents who want to break out on their own become angry at those who remind them of their old, dependent selves. Usually parents first and then teachers are the targets of this anger. Many adolescents will deliberately do the very thing to infuriate their parents because they want to establish their independence. These same adolescents may turn around and cry to their parents about a broken love affair the next week. The turbulence of adolescence in a changing and troubled culture can be trying to all involved.

According to Gisela Konopka's interviews, most adolescent women want to have close, mutually respectful relationships with parents and are hurt when their parents do not trust or respect them. These young women also reported that fears about sexuality were a major source of trouble between them and their parents: their parents feared that their daughters' social relations would lead to pregnancy.[26] This additional worry about pregnancy can create greater strains on the parent-daughter relationship than on the parent-son relationship. Parents may apply the double standard of sexual and social behavior to their sons and daughters. They may insist on limited sexual and social involvement for daughters, while allowing or even encouraging their adolescent sons to be somewhat independent and to "get experience," just as long as their girlfriends don't get pregnant. The injustice of this practice is experienced particularly clearly in families with both sons and daughters.

Sometimes the struggle between parents and daughters escalates into more than a family argument about curfews and sex. Of girls who are sent to youth houses or juvenile detention centers, a significant portion are there as "people in need of supervision" (PINS) and are sent by their parents who feel they cannot handle their daughters. Few boys are sent for detention in the PINS category because parents are less likely to be alarmed by a son who stays out till all hours of the night and engages in sexual intercourse.

Among some ethnic groups, a great deal of pressure is put on daughters to maintain a strict code of social and sexual behavior. For example, a good deal of conflict is experienced between newly immigrated Puerto Rican fathers and daughters. The daughter often wishes to have a relatively free and varied social life, as do most American teenagers. The father frequently feels that it is his personal responsibility to maintain his daughter's virginity. He may require her to keep very strict curfews, have chaperones on dates, even to return home from high school or college for lunch or an extended break. Since much of Latin American culture defines the woman's role as exclusively domestic, parents of Latin daughters in the United States may see schoolwork as secondary to their duties at home. While the Puerto Rican fathers may try to exert control over the social behavior of their sons, their attempts to control their daughters are much greater.[27]

Another source of tension between parents and their adolescent children is grades in school. Middle-class parents often strenuously push their adolescent sons toward school achievement. Since grades in high school qualify one for admission to college, and since college is the traditional route to professional training, the pressure to achieve is strong. Making the transition from the sports-minded youngster to the career-minded adult leaves the adolescent boy in a quandary. In fact, most boys do improve their grades in high school, but this is often viewed as a way to placate parents.

Parents give more mixed messages on achievement to their daughters. Middle-class parents may urge their daughters to get good marks in school, but the emphasis may be that good grades will help them find successful, achieving husbands. So girls continue getting good grades, but often for the sake of others, rather than for the self. Working-class parents are more likely to begin to downplay their daughers' academic achievement during the high school years, while middle-class parents are more likely to assume this stance once their daughters are in college. Many middle-class parents see college as a place for their daughters to meet "Mr. Right," so they may spend the money to send their daughters to college and insist that they perform well enough to complete their degrees. These same parents, however, may actively discourage their daughters from outstanding achievement, which parents fear may "scare away" potential husbands.[28]

Most parents , regardless of social class, race, or ethnic group, are concerned about the possible drug use, drinking, and criminal involvement of their adolescent children. While parents fear drug use and drinking for sons and daughters, they are particularly concerned that their sons will participate in violent interchanges, such as fighting, theft, burglary, and use of weapons. Violence and criminality are portrayed as supermasculine in the media, and what might have been a boy's fantasy can now be acted out with very serious consequences. Parents who raise their children in poor neighborhoods, and who are unemployed or marginally employed, may be particularly worried that their sons will give up on school and turn toward a life in "the streets."

Adolescents' relationships with their parents vary depending on many factors. One difference between working-class adolescents and their middle-class counterparts, according to a study by Lillian Rubin, is that working-class youth are more likely to live in their parents' home until they marry. White working-class adolescents often do not attend college, and if they do, they generally do not have the resources to go off and live on their own. For those who wish to leave their parents' home, marriage may be the only socially acceptable solution. One of Rubin's working-class women interviewees states: "When I think about it now, it sounds crazy, but honestly, the worse things got at home, the more I used to dream about how I was going to marry some good , kind, wise man who would take care of me; and how we'd have beautiful children; and how we'd live in our nice house; and how we'd always love each other and be happy."[29]

The working-class men and women in Rubin's study were expected to live at home and to contribute a good portion of their earnings to the family income until they married. In contrast, middle-class youth, regardless of sex, were more likely to attend college and live in a dormitory or apartment with friends and also possibly live on their own after college and before marriage. This brief period of freedom may make a small but significant difference. For middle-class males and females, living away from parents allows somewhat greater freedom and autonomy. It gives them the time and space to seek another perspective, as well as the possibility of coming into contact with people with nontraditional values that they may then choose to adopt for themselves. Most do not take this opportunity, but some do. This affords them greater access to and experience with nontraditional sex roles as compared to working-class youth. It should be noted, however, that while these class differences are important, people of all social classes continue to be influenced by the overwhelming societal agreement on sex-role definitions.

The Peer Group

During adolescence, the direct influence of the family declines. Many of the parents' most important values have already been learned by the young person, despite the differences that arise between parent and child. The adolescent now needs to develop an identity independent of her or his parents. Social relationships with friends are the "stage" on which this identity development is played out. The drama is often turbulent, the scene is constantly changing, and the star is frequently shifting in mood and persona.

The influence of friends—the peer group— varies somewhat across ethnic, racial, and social-class groups. For example, the influence of the peer group is greater for blacks than for whites, and greater for working-class and poor teenagers than for middle-class teenagers.[30] This is partly because a child is less likely to want to emulate parents whose lives are marked by social and economic deprivation and discrimination. It is unusual for adolescents to understand the social, economic, and political causes for their parents' situation. Teenagers from poor and working-class families may turn to the peer group in the neighborhood in an attempt to reject and avoid their parents' fates. Often this is in vain because the peer group does not have a strategy for changing the conditions of their social group's lives. Nonetheless, the peer group often has greater influence when adolescents reject their families as models for their own futures.

Partly because of early socialization experiences and cultural values, there are important differences in the structure, activities, roles, and values of male and female adolescent peer groups. While boys and girls often are part of the same crowd and even the same small clique within the larger crowd, adolescent girls and boys tend to have closest friends of their own sex and act differently with their friends. Males are usually expected to be more adventurous and aggressive while females are supposed to be more coquettish and passive.

Male-to-male interpersonal relationships are primarily activity-oriented. When "the boys" get together they usually are heavily engaged in sports. The emphasis on sports prowess can be obsessional for adolescent boys. Good athletes are awarded the highest social status. The proverbial football team captain gets acclaim from all. Young men may also play cards or share an activity such as working on a car. Males often brag about real or imagined sexual exploits and exaggeration is common. Masturbation is frequently discussed or practiced in a group, and sexual fantasies are often shared in great detail. The emphasis is on being "masculine," and this means physical, sexual, and social prowess.

For many young men, especially middle-class males, adolescence may be the first time the male peer group does not discourage school achievement. In preparation for future job responsibilities, middle-class males tend to improve their grades and become somewhat more academically ambitious, Peer support for academic work is generally present if not overwhelming, although school achievement is seen as more valuable if a young man is also a good athlete and is popular with young women. For working-class adolescents who do not have great expectations for job achievement, school success remains somewhat irrelevant. Many working-class and poor males drop out of school (officially or unofficially) as soon as possible and are not heavily criticized by their peers for this action.

Early socialization and present cultural values continue to limit the adolescent male. If a young man has personified his peer group's disdain for school early on and has never learned basic academic skills, he may suffer later in life. A young man who never learned to read in elementary school has described his wandering the halls and cutting classes in junior and senior high school as a reaction to panicking that, in class, his peers would discover that he still could not read. Instead he became a "tough guy." In fact, he was scared of being discovered.

The male peer group does not encourage young men to share emotions. Often adolescent males will be teased if they have too many anxieties about or deep feelings for a girlfriend or family member. At the very same time that young men, like young women, need to explore their emotions, the emphasis of the peer group and the larger society is that young men be tough, unemotional, and "cool." Although some ethnic groups permit more emotional expression by men than others,[31] most frequently a real sharing of feelings is not considered "masculine." This sets a pattern which is both difficult to change and dysfunctional for later relationships. Emotional expression is a healthy component of personality for all people. Men and women alike need to learn to express their feelings in order to get their own needs met and, later, to constructively show others, including their own children, that they love them. If men follow the traditionally "masculine" pattern and do not express their emotions, their children may view them as cold and unresponsive. Men may find it difficult to work through problems with their wives and close friends over the years.

Adolescent females, on the other hand, spend their time together sharing experiences, discussing feelings, friends, family, school, and boyfriends. The female peer group tends to emphasize popularity, especially with young men. Young women learn quickly how to be "one of the crowd." A female who pursues her own interests in reading or music, for example, may find herself isolated. Adolescent women engage in small group activities such as learning to dance, shopping, and some athletics. There is a great deal of group pressure to be "feminine": slim, attractive, a good listener, a supportive friend. Many of these characteristics are positive. They are, however, other-oriented, geared toward winning the approval of others.

While females are permitted to be "tomboys" in childhood, when they enter adolescence, women may be discouraged from developing their bodies for strength or athletic prowess. "Slimnastics" takes the place of the athletic skill building during this period. Although more and more young women are pursuing their interests in tennis, running, swimming, gymnastics, and figure skating, sports deemed less "feminine" (including most team sports) are more difficult for the adolescent woman to pursue because of social pressures. Recently, however, due partly to government pressure on colleges to distribute funds more equitably between women and men, more young women are defying the traditional pressures and are playing basketball, soccer, hockey, baseball, and football.

Female Flexibility

Although caring about others is a very positive virtue, and one that can be satisfying to women and men, the emphasis on the other-orientation is often so extreme for women that it can lead to a lack of personal definition, actions, and ambitions.[32] This is particularly true for white women. For adolescent women, this may translate into a distinct lack of support for academic achievement after high school. In college, young women are frequently told that boyfriends are more important than grades and that outstanding academic success will not lead to popularity. They often become less interested in school and less ambitious. During adolescence, young women become self-conscious about high achievement and their grades drop. Females continue, however, to do better than males do in school, since they can fall back on a fairly solid skill base developed during the preschool and elementary years. And adolescent girls are still interested in doing well enough not to displease their parents and teachers or lose favor with their friends. They do not want to make school an anxiety-provoking experience. But top achievement and success are avoided nonetheless. This ambivalent feeling about success in school has been described and measured by Matina Horner and named "fear of success."[33] Horner describes the bright, academically successful young woman in a bind: she wants to succeed, but success may conflict with her desire to be feminine and therefore popular. Horner has found that college women who imagine negative consequences to success hold back their best performance in a group of males and females, especially in competitive situations. Thus, these young women, fearing a loss of popularity or femininity, do not perform up to their potential. I repeated Horner's study with school-age boys and girls and found that "fear of success" begins to affect performance in girls in ninth grade and beyond; prior to that, girls' behavior or performance is not affected by their image of negative consequences of success.[34] My study, Horner's, Hoffman's,[35] and others indicate that while males can see the negative side of achievement or success, their performance is not affected by this view. Other researchers have found that females frequently "play dumb" on dates or try not to talk about subjects they know very well when they are with males who may not know as much.[36] These girls feel compelled to support the idea that a man must be a woman's intellectual superior in every area.

Judith Bardwick and Elizabeth Douvan explain these behaviors as typical of an ambivalence that characterizes white adolescent and adult women.[37] If a female is raised to believe that her most important role will be that of wife and mother, it will be important for her to keep her personality, interests, and desires as flexible and open as possible. When a prospective husband comes along, the young woman can then easily become whatever he wants her to be. If she has too many defined interests and abilities of her own, she may scare him away. Underlying this ambivalence is the societal value that females are not as important as males.

There are many problems inherent in this flexibility or ambivalence. The first is that clear personal identity, including realistic and positive information on the self, is necessary for all healthy people, male or female. Many women, most often those who are not employed outside the home, experience long periods of depression and personal anguish because they have not clarified their own identities.[38] Prince Charming may solve the temporary problem of a steady date but not the deep, lifelong problem of a stable personal identity and self-image. Women who marry young often go directly from their parents' home and supervision (or from a supervised college dormitory) to their husband's home and life-style. If they become pregnant soon, after the excitement dies down, they may find themselves lost in a sea of dinners, diapers, dusting, and dishes. Many women have spent years searching to discover their own interests, their own identities.

The feminine "wait and see" approach ignores the reality that most women spend the major part of their adult life doing paid work, not staying at home all day taking care of children. And a growing number of women, including ones with children, are the sole breadwinners in their families and live without men for long portions of their lives.[39] For young women, like young men, adolescence is the critical time to learn about one's abilities, interests, and energies, rather than to spend a great deal of time dreaming about a fantasy life of perfect marital bliss.

Most black females do not experience this syndrome of ambivalence in quite the same way as do their white counterparts. Peter Weston and Martha Mednick found that black college women exhibit much less fear of success than white college women.[40] In an extensive interview study, Joyce Ladner found that black working-class and poor adolescents highly value strength and resourcefulness in women; in addition, these young women choose independent and self-reliant women as their role models.[41] These differences in self-conception, motivations, and definitions of femininity arise from the reality of black women's lives. Because of severe economic discrimination and hardship, black women have historically found it necessary to be employed. The cultural value evolves to fit the economic and social necessities. Thus black adolescent women have somewhat different personal identities than their white counterparts, despite the fact that sex-role stereotypes exist for blacks, as well as whites, of all social classes. Among wealthy black adolescents, a more traditionally white version of femininity, emphasizing dependence and frailty, is more acceptable than it is among less wealthy black people.[42] If this example of the influence of economics on personal identity and values is any indication, one could expect more women of all races to shift their views of femininity toward independence and resourcefulness. With inflation, and growing economic insecurity, most people's buying power is decreasing and more and more women therefore need to be employed.

High School

High schools give adolescents a glimpse of what their future roles in and relationships with societal institutions will be. While schools are supposed to encourage all students to strive to fulfill themselves, officials who make school policies will often define that "fulfillment" in sex-typical terms. This kind of "tracking" is different for people of various races and social classes.

Although Title IX of the 1972 Education Amendments has made it illegal to sex-segregate classes, many schools continue discriminatory practices. Since high schools help to train young adults for their future work, and often subscribe to traditional notions of appropriate male and female adult roles, they may encourage girls to take courses in home economics, typing, stenography, or bookkeeping, while encouraging boys to take courses in metalwork, carpentry, and auto mechanics. In the past, watered-down versions of these classes have been given cross-sex—for example, "Cooking for Bachelors" and "Home Repair for Housewives."

Physical education and athletic programs offer one of the most glaring examples of differential treatment of males and females in schools. In high schools and colleges in the United States, the average amount of money spent on female athletics is, at best, ten percent that spent on male athletics. Some schools create equal treatment and expenditures on paper but fail to advertise or recruit students to new sex-integrated programs. Some even harass students who try to get into non-sex-typical programs.

High school counselors, many with the best of intentions, may encourage students to sign up for courses or go into fields deemed appropriate for someone of their sex, race, and social class. Counselors encourage what they believe to be *realistic* for an individual; but there is a catch, a self-fulfilling prophecy. For example, a counselor tells a student, "Go into teaching, it's a good job for a woman." The young woman becomes a teacher and feels positively about it. Does this prove the counselor right? Or is it possible that the young woman had no idea of other alternatives that may have been even more fulfilling for her than teaching? When the counselor looks back and sees so many former female students as teachers, does it strengthen the belief that women naturally love teaching, or does the counselor question whether the young females perceived any choice in the matter? Most people prefer to view themselves as essentially correct, and this fictitious counselor may be no different. The counselor may give the next group of female students the same advice, insisting that "so many girls are happy as teachers," and so the limited choices continue. Counselors probably find it easier to handle the large number of students they have by categorizing them. Due to discrimination and shared group experiences, categories such as sex, race, and social class are, unfortunately, usually the best predictors of who will end up in what kinds of jobs. The counselor may thus use these categories as a "realistic" way to get through a too-large case load of students.

Sometimes high schools are sex-segregated and deny women and men opportunities to pursue subjects that are considered "unsuitable" for their sex. Before the existence of Title IX, Alice de Rivera filed a court suit against the New York City Board of Education and won the right to attend a previously all-male math- and science-oriented high school. She says of her struggle to get academic training:

Aside from being discouraged to study for a career, women are discouraged from preparing for jobs involving anything but secretarial work, beauty care, nursing, cooking, and the fashion industry. During my fight over Stuyvesant [High School] I investigated the whole high school scene, and found that out of the twenty-seven vocational high schools in the city, only seven are co-ed. The boys' vocational schools teach trades in electronics, plumbing, carpentry, foods, printing...etc. The girls are taught to be beauticians, secretaries, or health aides. This means that if a girl is seeking entrance to a vocational school, she is pressured to feel that certain jobs are masculine and others feminine. She is forced to conform to the Board of Education's image of her sex. At the seven co-ed vocational schools, boys can learn clerical work, food preparation, and beauty care along with the girls. But the courses that would normally be found in a boys' school are not open to girls. There are only two schools where a girl can prepare for a "masculine" job.[43]

Even academic achievement tests, which are often used to place students in special classes or schools, contribute to the sex-role stereotyping of academic abilities and interests. For example, educators have long assumed that girls are less competent in mathematics, spatial relations, and analytic skills. Yet research shows that once the content of math achievement tests is translated into problems that are perceived as sex-appropriate for females, for example ones involving baking and pattern-making rather than military events, few if any differences in ability between the sexes can be found.[44] Most math achievement tests, however, include examples that are considered masculine. Achievement tests do not, in any event, test innate ability. Research indicates that sex differences in certain analytic skills do not exist if the males and females being studied have had equivalent formal and informal training.[45] Similarly, standardized tests that are supposed to measure verbal or mathematical "aptitude" are also biased. They tend to be based on the experience of white middle-class people and to make experiences of minority, working-class, or poor people work against them in the testing situation.

The schools' tracking system has well-trained accomplices among adolescents themselves. Adolescents' expectations and their willingness to fulfill these expectations arise out of their perceptions of what is possible for people like them, be they male or female; black, white, or Hispanic; wealthy or working class. If adolescents are members of a group that has a high unemployment rate or limited educational opportunity, it is less likely that they will train for and expect to be in high-status jobs in adulthood. Although most people want to improve their lives over those of their parents, change on this individual level often is impossible. So adolescence may become a training ground that helps to prepare children to enter a world similar to that of their parents. Middle-class students usually prepare by going to college. The young men plan to be businessmen, doctors, lawyers, engineers; the young women plan to be teachers and social workers, jobs that are considered "nurturing" and that are thus consistent with the feminine ideal. Working-class students frequently prepare by going to trade school and learning a skill: the young men train to be mechanics, electricians, plumbers; the young women, to be secretaries. Students from poor families often prepare by taking odd jobs. The males may look for a break or develop a "hustle"; the females may get pregnant and leave school or the job market. Often, the street style covers an underlying depression about what society has to offer. Although there are obviously many exceptions to the above generalizations, adolescents often "willingly choose" school programs and future vocational roles that will lead them right back into the social position of their parents. All those years of training to know their particular sex role, racial stereotype, and social-class position "pay off" in the form of submission to "tracking" for future occupations.[46]

Curriculum and reading materials for high school students, like those for preschool and elementary school children, reinforce sex-role stereotypes. For example, most history books focus almost entirely on male achievement. Strict sex-role definitions in the past restricted access to non-sex-typical positions and training and thus drastically limited the number of "history-making" women. There has been a bias against regarding women's activities as important enough to be recorded as "history" and put in texts. And in addition, non-sex-typical behavior on the part of either men or women has often been regarded as deviant and therefore not worthy of mention. Most history books describe men as competitive and brave, fighters and statesmen, while women are portrayed as passive seamstresses (Betsy Ross) or famous men's wives. Although many American history texts include at least a few sentences about Susan B. Anthony, very few books fully discuss women's important work throughout history—for example, fighting against slavery and for improved working conditions for women and men. Similar omissions can be found in texts for English, science, math, and home economics courses as well. The "invisibility" of women in textbooks is paralleled by the "invisibility" of blacks, Hispanics, and other minorities; working-class and poor people; and gay men and lesbians.[47]

The problems in the school curriculum are often not the fault of the classroom teacher, who functions under many constraints. A teacher with overcrowded classes may find it barely possible to keep up with class preparation and grading. Difficult working conditions may make it hard for teachers to research non-sex-typical educational materials on their own. They usually must rely on texts that have been around for a long time and reflect old prejudices. Frequently, there is no money to buy new books.

Student groups and teacher groups, especially if they work together, can influence the types of materials and courses offered in high schools. At John Dewey High School in Brooklyn, New York, one such club exists. Its name is FIRE (Feminists Intent on Recognizing Equality) and it has succeeded in raising questions about sex stereotyping in the curriculum and about the lack of female administrators. Not incidentally, John Dewey High School has a popular and high-quality women's studies program.

The model provided by a high school's faculty and administration also reinforces traditional sex-role patterns. As the level of education increases, so does the proportion of male compared to female teachers and administrators. In most high schools, there are slightly more male teachers than female teachers. More important, most men are found in math, science, history, and shop departments and most women teach English, music, art, and home economics. And 96 percent of the secondary school administrators are men.[48]

Higher Education

While college and university students are usually considered adults in legal terms, most who enter college directly after high school remain dependent on their parents for at least financial support and often for emotional and moral support in making important decisions. The college student is really caught between the dependency of adolescence and impending adulthood. College education for men is usually seen as a way to get a better-paying and more interesting job. For women, college education has the same function, but often women's expected role as homemaker undermines the seriousness with which they are viewed as students, by both others and themselves. A larger proportion of females graduate from high school and get better grades compared to males. There are, therefore, more females qualified to go to college than males. In 1978, for the first time, women outnumbered men in college, making up 52 percent of the undergraduate population. However, a smaller percentage of qualified females goes to and completes college, as compared to qualified males. According to a recent study, out of the qualified male group, 65 percent entered college and 45 percent graduated; of qualified females, 50 percent went to college and 30 percent graduated.[49]

External barriers help to discourage women from continuing their education. Women have been discriminated against in admission to and scholarships for college and graduate school. Until 1972, when Title IX of the Education Amendments mandated that schools and colleges supported by federal tax dollars had to offer men and women equal opportunity to learn skills, advance, choose an area of study, play a sport, or win a scholarship, discrimination was blatant. Bernice Sandler gave the following testimony on sex discrimination in higher education before the Judiciary Committee of the U.S. House of Representatives in 1971.

For the last decade at the University of Michigan, according to C. G. Wilson, Executive Associate Director of Admissions, the Office of Admissions has "adjusted" requirements to ensure that an "overbalance"—that is, a majority— of women would not occur in the freshman class for a number of years, despite the fact that in terms of grades and test scores, there are more qualified female applicants than males. At Pennsylvania State University, an artificial ratio of 2.5 men to every female is deliberately maintained. . . . In graduate school, the quota system is even more vicious. At Stanford, for example, the proportion of women students has declined over the last ten years, even though more and equally or better qualified women have applied for admission to graduate school. (One out of every 2.8 men who applied was accepted; only 1 woman out of 4.7 applicants was accepted.)[50]

Although Title IX makes sex discrimination illegal, enforcement of the law is sporadic, and litigation against colleges and universities takes several years to conclude. Thus some discriminatory practices continue.

Once women and men do enter college, they are likely to find the curriculum male-focused, as it was in high school. Even in areas of study that are considered to be "feminine," such as literature, required courses frequently include only peripheral references to women. In recent years, women's studies courses that focus on women in history, literature, the arts, and the natural and social sciences have begun to counter the male bias of the curriculum. Today almost all colleges and universities offer at least one women's studies course, and 330 campuses have women's studies programs.[51]

As in high school, tracking according to sex occurs throughout higher education. Although some change occurred in the 1970s, women are still more likely than men to major in education, nursing, and humanities, while men are more likely to major in natural sciences or business and to be enrolled in premedical, prelaw, or predental programs. The "male-dominated" majors lead to fairly high-paying, prestigious, and high-pressure jobs compared to most of the "female-dominated" majors. Miriam Gilbert explains that many young women who are interested in natural and medical sciences are encouraged to take a nursing program because it is socially acceptable, while some less motivated males feel compelled to attempt to achieve the "supermasculine" status of medical doctor. The pressure on both males and females to enter professions typical for their sex is great.[52] The now-familiar message comes to college students through advice and expectations created by their professors, advisors, peers, family, and the media. Each field of study in turn influences and socializes its students. Education and psychology students may learn to be more aware of and sensitive to others' thoughts and feelings. Natural science and prelaw courses are likely to encourage competitive, individualistic, and aggressive behavior. One's choice of major then has an ongoing socializing influence on the individual (usually consistent with one's socially defined sex role).

The structure of colleges and universities themselves, plus the role models available, add to the ongoing sex-role socialization of students. In colleges and universities, according to a 1977 study, of all administrators, 79 percent were white men, 14 percent were white women, 5 percent were minority men, and 2 percent were minority women.[53] At the end of the 1970s, less than 25 percent of college faculty members were women, and they were mostly in the lower ranks of instructor or assistant professor. Between 1974 and 1975, the percentage of women in the highest ranks of professor and associate professor actually declined.[54]

Students again see that people in high-powered jobs are generally male.[55] This puts pressure on male students to achieve and on female students to hold back. With new affirmative action laws in the early 1970s, more women (and minority) faculty were hired. This significantly increased the number of women college and university professors. However, beginning in 1975 most American colleges and universities experienced severe budget cuts, and large numbers of newly hired faculty were laid off or fired. This means that women and minority students will continue to be deprived of important role models.

Participation in student activities is often a training ground for later job skills and contacts. Being the editor of a college newspaper is good journalism training; often college newspaper experience is counted by professional newspapers and magazines and college editors may be offered jobs. Participating in student government helps one develop speaking skills, facilitates entry into law school, and helps to build personal contacts for later business or professional life. These top student leadership roles have been likely to go to male students. The buddy, fraternity, or club system which often influences these selections has usually excluded women students.[56]

Internal factors also influence college, graduate school, and professional achievement. Females are more likely to fear top achievement and shy away from the most competitive areas. Mirra Komarovsky reports that many of the college women she interviewed admitted lying to their dates about good grades and "playing dumb" in order not to scare their boyfriends away. The college men in Komarovsky's study said that they preferred to be the intellectual "heavy" or leader compared to their girlfriends, despite their desire to have intelligent dates.[57] According to Alice Rossi, the characteristics seen as most important to being a scientist (or other highly paid professional) are high intellectual ability, intense channeling of energy in one direction, extreme independence, and distance from others. These very characteristics are anathema to traditional femininity.[58] While female college students are indeed highly motivated, interested, and capable, they carry the handicap of knowing that their broad social acceptability will most probably be based on their marriageability, not on their own educational or intellectual achievement. This may keep women from striving to achieve in certain areas. Males have the dubious advantage of having their educational and occupational advancement as central to their social acceptance and sense of self-worth. The young man who is not particularly motivated toward high marks and high-pressure jobs may receive scorn from others for not being "masculine" enough. Many young men experience serious psychosomatic problems in college in response to these pressures to perform "like a man."

In colleges, many lesbians and gay men also experience a form of "fear of success" which is related to self-exposure. Homosexuals may fear that academic (and later career) success may force them either to be disclosed as gay and then rejected or to live a double life, keeping their sexual preference hidden from their academic or professional colleagues. The increasing number of successful academic and professional lesbians and gay men who are public about their sexual preferences makes it more acceptable and comfortable for other gays to openly seek success.

Despite the fact that internal barriers to achievement do exist, in many colleges and graduate and professional schools, once the external barriers are lifted, more and more men and women choose traditionally cross-sex-typical training and future jobs. When, in the recent past, elementary and high school teaching went from being an extremely low-paying job to a moderate-paying job, many men became teachers. When working with children could also allow men to earn a reasonable living, many men overcame social and internalized objections to their performing this type of job. Beginning in the 1970s, as medical and law schools were forced to cease discriminating against women in admissions, many motivated and capable females successfully entered these fields. From 1900 to 1970, the percentage of women admitted to law and medical schools remained below 10 percent; in the late 1970s, 25 percent of the entering class of medical students and over 30 percent of the entering class of law students were women. Internal barriers show a remarkable tendency to fade (faster for some than for others) once their support from external barriers diminishes.[59]

FIVE:
Young Adulthood

Decisions and Responsibilities

YOUNG ADULTHOOD IS A TIME when women and men begin to leave behind the limited responsibilities and major dependencies of adolescence and establish definitions of themselves

which are relatively enduring. This period does not necessarily begin on a particular birthday or start with a physical event. The time when one assumes ultimate responsibility for oneself and one's actions depends on many factors. Many people who go to college or graduate school remain financially dependent upon their parents well into their twenties. Some people will assume total responsibility for themselves in their mid-teens. Much depends upon the individual and his or her social milieu. Middle-class people tend to become financially independent of their families later than working-class or poor youth, largely because they are more likely to go on to college and need their

parents' aid to do so; their parents are also more able to provide this support. However, financial independence is not the only sign of adulthood. Making important life choices on one's own marks the real beginning of adulthood.

Who and what people choose to become will greatly reflect what they have come to see as appropriate and possible. They are influenced by both prior socialization and by how they perceive the future. In the contemporary United States, a large array of alternatives appears to exist. An increasing number of women and men are choosing jobs, life-styles, and family patterns which are counter to the traditional sex roles. Recent studies indicate that an overall shift in values toward blending sex roles has occurred. More people are seeing the importance of androgyny— of women and men both having some traditionally masculine and some traditionally feminine characteristics. Compared with previous generations, more young women are preparing them- selves for future jobs which will be satisfying and pay relatively well, while more young men indicate an interest in spending time with their children.[1]

Nonetheless, the ongoing strength of the cultural values expressed by traditional sex roles should not be underestimated. Sex roles are mightily persistent despite the fact that there is more support than ever to make nontraditional choices. But those who do choose traditional life-styles are now more aware that they too are making choices and selecting options they hope will prove to be fulfilling in their own lives.

People make life choices on the basis of what they think will satisfy them. What ingredients make for satisfaction or happiness over a long-term period in a changing world? Surveys of women and men from various backgrounds indicate that people are most satisfied when they have some direct control over their own lives and when they derive self-esteem from their work.[2] These two criteria are crucial in chosing future life-styles and jobs. Whether and how one achieves these two goals depends, to some degree, on the background, experiences, and opportunities of the individual in question.

While almost all social-class, ethnic, and racial groups see child rearing as the primary responsibility of women and breadwinning as the major task of men, groups differ on the exclusivity of these domains and on the timing of these events. As discussed earlier, most of the particular ethnic or racial group differences tend to dissolve once middle-class status is attained. Economic and social mobility diminishes the influence of our historical and cultural backgrounds and tends to homogenize us.[3]

Class differences in sex-role behavior are complex. Middle-class people are more likely to espouse an androgynous point of view compared to working-class people. For example, most middle-class people say that women should be educated and have careers of their own and that men should participate somewhat in raising their children; yet they still think it is ultimately a woman's responsibility to care for home and children, especially when children are young, and a man's responsibility to bring in the major part of the family income. When a problem with the children arises, it is usually seen as the wife's fault, and when money problems arise, the husband is usually blamed. Working-class people are less likely to believe, abstractly, in androgenous ideals.[4] Yet the economic necessity for the wife to work outside the home (and the lack of funds to pay someone else to do household work) increases the likelihood that the working-class husband will engage in domestic tasks.

Many working-class young adults see fewer options for themselves as compared to their middle-class counterparts. Educational opportunity and encouragement; availability of alternative role models; money to support further education, travel, or business ventures; and interesting and fulfilling job opportunities are much more limited for working-class people. With fewer options (both real and perceived), the working-class adult is more likely to see young adulthood as a period of "settling in," of developing as tight a sense of security as possible, of continuing to be very close to family and old friends, and of specializing family work and paid work by sex.

During young adulthood, people make life choices which are often based on sex-role-stereotypical ideas. These decisions are not *necessarily* harmful to the individual. Yet they sometimes close off other life choices and limit alternatives. A woman's decision to become a mother at a young age, or man's decision to focus all of his energy on his job, can have serious lifelong implications.

Such choices are logical, if sometimes extreme, extensions of the traditional male and female roles. Most men do, in fact, pursue the masculine role, even though their pursuit of it is often a major source of strain for them.[5] Most married women are happier if they are not exclusively tied into the role of wife and mother and have other outside work or interests. Yet many women feel guilty about not being totally enthralled with the housewife role.[6] Why do people keep striving to be supermasculine or superfeminine if these roles are not necessarily satisfying? Part of the answer is a "cultural lag." This occurs when economic and other social-structural changes occur, yet cultural values (and hence our deepest feelings) remain the same. Increasingly, married women must work outside the home to help their families survive economically. And with longer life expectancy and fewer children per family, most women will spend at least half of their adult lives without any children living at home. People who are tied to extreme feminine or extreme masculine roles may be suffering the strains of somewhat anachronistic personalities.

The times require greater sex-role blending and sharing, and most people are, in fact, moving in that direction. The shifting consciousness about sex roles is both influenced by and influences economic and social changes. The women's movement of the late 1960s and 1970s made millions of people aware of the constricting nature of traditional sex roles and the sharp differences in power between men and women in American society. This new consciousness has motivated many women and some men to question their roles, to speak out for changes in the society, and to effect some of these changes through political, social, and personal action. This new consciousness has altered many people's self-understanding and expectations, whether they consider themselves to be supporters of the women's movement or not. It has also altered some concrete conditions affecting educational and employment opportunity as well as reproductive rights and marriage. Legislation has been passed, some on a federal and some on a state or local level, mandating equal pay for equal work, limiting employment and education discrimination, legalizing abortion, limiting forced sterilizations, liberalizing divorce laws, forbidding discrimination against lesbians and gay men, and changing athletic and academic programing in schools. Although these laws are not always effective and do not exist in all localities, they are important nonetheless. A person's sex-role behavior is deeply influenced by the organization and ideology of the society. While a new consciousness helps change the organization of the society, economic and social changes further alter consciousness. The two change together.[7]

Marriage

Most young adults in the contemporary United States marry. Yet more people are breaking away from this pattern and making other choices. Many more people cohabit or live together without marriage, either temporarily or permanently. More individuals live in homosexual relationships. Others choose to remain single, with or without children. Even among those who do marry, many arrange their family responsibilities in different ways than their parents did. Today people marry at a somewhat later age than in the recent past. A small but significant number of couples delay having children, sometimes until their thirties.[8] Why do people make the life choices they do?

Almost all people who choose an ongoing sexual-emotional, love relationship hope that the relationship will yield affection, support, sexual fulfillment, and the sharing of joys, woes, activities, and responsibilities. In addition, those who marry codify their relationship, possibly to achieve adult status, to provide a legalized parental relationship for children they plan to have, or to satisfy pressuring parents who want their young adult children to be "taken care of."[9] To most people in our society, marriage represents a level of maturity or independence which has a legal label and is therefore publicly recognizable.

Most young unmarried people, particularly heterosexual women, have an extremely romanticized view of marriage. This image is propagated by romance magazines, Hollywood, and wishful thinking. Some people "fall" into marriage: they marry the person they are dating because they believe that marriage is the next logical and required step for an individual of their age and social circumstances. This view is more often held by men than women. After a short period of time, what may be a blissful union must face the harsh realities of life: economic insecurity, sharing space and time extensively with another person, conflicts over individual habits, disagreements over values and choices, sexual adjustments, bad moods, and so on. Some problems are more important than others, but all require adjustments. As in steady dating, traditional sex-role behavior is likely to increase upon marriage. Because the stakes are higher, traditional sex roles become even more rigid in marriage. Parents and in-laws often involve themselves in the relationship and make their usually traditional views known. The society in general views and judges married people as a unit—a couple. A couple needs to make important life decisions. Wife and husband decide how to earn their livings, where to live, and if and when to have children. The newly married adults must decide on their level of involvement with their parents, their friends, their community, their work. Young married women often assume (and are socially assigned) the primary responsibility for housekeeping, cooking, and keeping up social and family contacts. They also generally feel primary responsibility for keeping the marriage happy and intact. The young married man is apt to believe that he must earn a solid living for his new family and that he must wield a large amount of authority in marital decisions.

But what's wrong with the traditional marriage where each participant knows and accepts her or his particular role? The skyrocketing divorce rate (more than one in three marriages in the United States ends in divorce) implies at least some negative aspects of marriage as an institution and of traditional marriage roles. Marriage is often seen as the answer to life's problems; in fact, it creates at least as many problems as it solves. A number of studies done over the last twenty-five years suggest that women and men see marriage and are affected by it differently. Researchers indicate that married women report more marital problems than their husbands do. Many women report a lack of communication with and support from their husbands.[10] Many more married women than married men feel inadequate and have poor self-images. Compared to single women and married men of comparable ages, married women tend to experience more personality problems such as passivity, phobic tendencies, depression, irrational fears, and other neurotic symptoms. Interestingly enough, single men are more likely to experience these personality problems than either married men or, for most of the problems, single women.[11] Some researchers conclude that marriage is a more favorable institution for men than it is for women. Eli Zaretsky claims that the role of the wife in our society is particularly difficult because she is required to set up a haven or happy retreat from the rest of the world. With increasing pressures on men and women to make ends meet, with unemployment and poor job opportunities making economic support harder, and with children's increasing exposure to drug abuse and violence, creating that haven at home becomes more and more difficult.[12] In addition, most wives in traditional sex-role-defined marriages have significantly less power and authority than their husbands, even at home. This leaves traditional wives in the bind of being responsible for family satisfaction, but not fully able to make their own decisions. A twenty-nine-year-old mother of three states:

He just goes to work and brings some money home, but I have all the responsibilities. I tell him what the bills are. I know when there's not enough money to pay them all. I know when something's wrong in the family. I know when his brother and sister-in-law are splitting up. I know when his mother's unhappy. I know when there's a problem with the kids. Why, I'm even the one who knows when there's a problem in our marriage. I have to tell him about all those things and most of the time he just listens to a few words and tunes it out. I'm the one who knows about it, and I'm the one who gets stuck worrying what to do about it.[13]

Because the housewife earns no money of her own in exchange for her labor, her work and her being are often devalued. Earning no salary can make the housewife feel degraded and out of the mainstream of economic life. In addition, the housewife's work is "never done." She is always "on call," always at her workplace, never on vacation. She's a twenty-four-hour-a-day, every day worker with only room, board, clothing, and perhaps some "pocket money" for pay. Finally, a housewife's work is very difficult to judge. Has she raised her children properly? It may take years (or be impossible) to find that out. Is she a good wife to her husband? There is no Christmas or productivity bonus, no chance for promotion on her job. So the housewife is never really sure if she's good at what she's working so hard at.[14]

Even though studies show that the married man may suffer less from a poor self image than the married woman, he has other problems. He is under great pressure (from others and himself) to support his family economically. If he is unable to handily provide for his family, he may feel like a failure.[15] Many jobs do not pay well enough nor are they intrinsically interesting. Most men, like most women, have jobs that are heavily supervised and repetitive. With little control and self-esteem from their jobs, many people feel unsatisfied in their work lives. For men, the traditional model is that work is the core of life. If the core is disappointing, it will be hard to compensate for. With masculinity measured by the size of a paycheck,[16] the drive to be masculine can lead to obsessive worrying about money and work. When a husband is unhappy with his job, marital satisfaction is likely to decline. Many sociologists believe that men's sense of failure in living up to the masculine ideal is a major factor in creating marital instability among poor people.[17] Men may also suffer because they did not receive childhood training that encourages involvement with children or closeness with loved ones. While men have friends with whom they may share athletic interests or drinks at the corner bar, often their needs for closeness, intimacy, and love are not met. For example, American fathers spend an average of twelve minutes per day with their children.[18]

A particularly grim expression of dissatisfaction with life and marriage is that of family violence in general and wife battering in particular. Estimates are that from 10 to 33 percent of all husbands engage in wife battering. This partly reflects the relative powerlessness of women, their dependence on men, an ideology of ownership of the woman by her man, and the widespread use of violence in our society. Until recently, wife battering was either laughed at or ignored by the legal authorities. Many police and court personnel perceived it to be normal. Attitudes toward wife battering have changed somewhat, due to publicity and political action on the part of women's groups. Shelters and other support services for battered women and their children have emerged all over the country, although they are few in number and poorly funded. Some training courses have helped to change police attitudes and practices to some degree. Overall, a great deal of public information has been generated which makes wife battering less socially acceptable than it has been. It remains, however, one of the most serious social problems of our time.[19] Marital rape and the raping of teenage girls by fathers, brothers, uncles, or "friends" of the family is also widespread. These forms of family violence, complex in their origin, grow out of rigid and traditional sex-role patterns.

Married life, of course, can also be very satisfying. Many people develop loving, caring, and respectful relationships with their spouses. Most likely they work hard at maintaining and developing their marriages. They probably learn how to articulate their needs to their partners, and they may have the social support of a network of family and friends.

Single Life

In many ways a nonmarried life-style choice is defiant of traditional sex roles. While this is not always the case, people who remain single may be rejecting the sex-role scripts that they have been trained to recite.

According to interview studies and survey research, a nonmarried life-style is not usually an unhappy or neurotic one. This is particularly true for individuals who feel they have independently chosen their life-styles rather than simply accepted them. Single individuals, especially women, are likely to describe themselves as well-adjusted individuals with normal self-esteem. Contrary to popular mythology, single women tend to be happier than single men, primarily because they have had the childhood socialization to get more of their social and personal needs met.[20] Women tend to have particularly close and sustaining relationships with their women friends. For the single woman, close friends provide much of the support and companionship that others find in marriage. Single people usually make commitments to friends and to work which can be very satisfying.

Lesbianism and Male Homosexuality

During young adulthood, lesbians and gay men experience changes in developmental goals similar to those of their heterosexual counterparts. Their search for friends, social support, and continuity is often longer and more arduous than the standard heterosexual search. This is due to the general "invisibility" of gays in our heterosexually dominant society as well as to homophobia—the extreme fear of lesbians and gay men.

Research suggests that those lesbians and gay men who find social supports lead relatively happy lives; their personalities, types of employment, and social views are very varied. Most gay people seek long-term, close, loving relationships. In a study of thousands of lesbians and gay men (the vast majority of whom were white) over 75 percent of the lesbians and over 60 percent of the gay men reported living with their lovers; the majority reported getting love, warmth, and friendship from their partners. For lesbians, the importance of living and sharing a life with a lover is very important, more so than for male gays in general. Lesbians are more likely to have long-term relationships and to have strong emotional ties to their lovers (whether or not they end up in long-term relationships) compared to male gays. These differences between men and women with homosexual preferences reflect traditional sex-role differences within our society.[21]

Yet lesbians and gay men are somewhat different from their heterosexual counterparts in a number of important ways. Many gays seek more egalitarian relationships than they see as possible or likely in heterosexual relationships. In one study, lesbians were found to be more autonomous, spontaneous, oriented toward the future rather than the past, and otherwise as well adjusted as were heterosexual women. The researcher interprets these results to indicate that while it is possible that women with these characteristics are attracted to other women to begin with, it is likely that once a woman realizes her lesbianism, she also realizes she will have to rely on herself rather than on a man. Thus, she is likely to develop these adaptive characteristics.[22]

Many lesbians and gay men clarify their sexual identities in young adulthood or later. This means that they carry with them the remnants of their earlier heterosexual experience. In one study involving interviews of thousands of gay people, over one third of the lesbians and under one fifth of the gay men had been married: in both cases slightly over half had children from those marriages. These statistics give a small indication of the extent to which many lesbians and gay men struggle trying to fit into and conform to heterosexual expectations before coming to accept and appreciate their own sexual preferences.[23]

While choices of lesbianism or male homosexuality may be highly fulfilling, the individuals making these choices often face a great deal of social pressure and criticism. In addition to the standard strains in establishing meaningful love relationships and a sense of community support, gay adults may feel threatened by a perceived need for secrecy. Lesbians and gay men sometimes fear their lovers will return to a heterosexual preference, feel stresses due to a lack of role definitions within the couple, or have difficulty in handling their children's reaction to their homosexuality. The lesbian couple striving to create a loving and supportive partnership does not generally receive the acknowledgment and respect afforded a heterosexual couple. Difficulty may arise in bringing a lover home to meet parents or to an office party to meet workmates. Additionally, lesbians and gay men experience discrimination in employment and housing as well as potential physical threats from violently antigay individuals or groups.[24]

Studies of lesbians and gay men repeatedly indicate that closeting one's homosexuality can lead to serious problems. While "coming out" certainly decreases the strain, and allows individuals to develop more respect for themselves and from others, a society which feels threatened by nontraditional sexuality makes its values known.

Our society perpetuates myths about the basic unhappiness or even sickness of single people, lesbians, male gays, and others who do not follow the traditional sex-role pattern. These myths, part of our sex-role socialization, may scare some people into traditional choices. And those who question and defy traditional sex roles often have to battle not only the criticism of others but also their own internalized fears and stereotypes. Even among the most nontraditional people, remnants of sex-role socialization remain, and doubts about one's own judgments arise. Self-confidence, determination, and help from others facilitates successful nontraditional as well as traditional choices. The last decade has witnessed the growth of organizations and informal support groups for people choosing nontraditional life-styles. These groups serve the dual purpose of supporting individuals in their life choices (by providing networks of friends and companions) and of creating changes in the social, legal, and political milieu.

Deciding to Have Children

Why do people have children? Many people do not, in fact, *decide* to have children—they just have them. Some women and men never consider the alternative of not becoming parents. Some women become pregnant by accident, decide not to have an abortion, and keep the baby. Others make a conscious choice to have or not have children. Lois Hoffman and Martin Hoffman suggest some of the many reasons people want to have children. Children may help one achieve adult status and social identity; for women this is linked to the idea that motherhood is woman's central role. Having children may give an adult a sense of "immortality." Some people have children for religious reasons. Some have children because they want affectionate family ties or because they believe children will be stimulating and fun. Having children can give one a sense of achievement, competence, creativity, or power. People also have children because it is socially acceptable, or because children will look after their parents in their old age.[25]

A growing number of teenage girls are having babies, both in and out of the confines of marriage. In the United States in the mid-1970s, approximately 600,000 babies were born to teenage mothers every year.[26] While having a baby makes one feel adult at first, it is a major responsibility which serves to limit future choices. Because maternity is seen as the height of femininity in our society, many young women have babies in order to settle on a clearly feminine identity. Erik Erikson calls this type of choice "identity foreclosure" because it serves to solidify an identity well before other possibilities and choices have been explored.[27] What may be good at eighteen isn't necessarily satisfying at twenty-five. This may be true of all choices, but having a baby is irreversible. Young women with children may have many difficulties. They are in a particularly weak position in establishing long-term relationships with men. Children who are not planned for often are the cause of arguments and deep-seated resentments between parents who may be struggling to keep the family afloat. Teenage marriages with young children tend to be quite unstable. Young women with children are also unlikely to develop job skills which may offer other economic and social options to them later on. They are generally extremely dependent upon those who economically support them—their men, families, or the government— and are likely to suffer abuse from these same individuals or agents. Many teenage mothers feel a particular lack of control over their lives and often have few sources of self-esteem—the key ingredients to satisfaction.[28]

More and more people are considering what it means to become a parent before they decide whether or not to have children. In an attempt to discover the bases on which people decide about having children, the Boston Women's Health Book Collective interviewed a large number of adults and asked them about their reasons for having or not having a child. One man said:

I think kids are mind-expanding. That's one reason why I know I would have kids, because if I didn't there'd be a whole chunk missing. It's a very basic human experience that you've already experienced as a child and now you experience as a parent.[29]

Another person adds:

I want to have a baby. We want to have a baby together. It's the next stage in our relationship and we just feel like we're ready to share our love with a new person, one who's part of both of us.[30]

Although most people have children, others decide not to, sometimes because of the things they would have to give up. A man in his thirties says:

I just don't want to put my energy into raising children for twenty years. I want to put my energies into the organizations I'm in. I want to make some difference in society, so that things might be a little bit different because I lived.[31]

Another person states:

The fact is we're severely overpopulated. So there's really no reason to have a child unless you know you really enjoy the process of raising one. Not because you have some tremendous expectations for it: it's going to do the things you never did; it's going to love you because it has to. No. The only reason to have one is because you really enjoy the process of raising a child.[32]

People who choose not to have children believe their needs for achievement, influence, immortality, excitement, and loving relationships can be met through other personal relationships; careers; and work in community, political, and social organizations. Those who choose not to have children do not necessarily dislike children. Some people who are particularly interested in children, such as teachers, prefer not to be with children at home as well as at work; they may desire to have close relationships with many children over the years and spend more free time with other adults or by themselves. A middle-aged woman states:

It's too bad that young women think that they have to have children in order to be "fulfilled." I'm fifty-six, never had kids, and feel as "fulfilled" as I could possibly be. Our lives can be rich with work, friends, other people's children and many other things. I don't think motherhood is the right choice for every woman.[33]

There have always been some people who have chosen not to have children. In the past, many of those people have felt compelled to remain single or sexually inactive because of a lack of adequate birth control. Now there is more social support for remaining childless; there are even organizations that help people deal with social pressures to have children.[34] A study of women in their twenties and thirties compared those who planned to have children with those who planned not to. They found the two groups of women to be equally mentally healthy and satisfied. The women who planned not to have children reported greater involvement with work and community activities.[35]

Children have a major— and sometimes negative—effect on marital relationships. Joseph Veroff and Sheila Feld interviewed hundreds of couples and found that those without children tended to be more satisfied with their relationships than those with children.[36] This may be due to the presence of a stronger personal relationship to begin with between couples who choose to be childless. It may also be due to the fact that they don't have children. A number of studies indicate that most marital problems begin to emerge with the birth of the first child. Having an infant at home puts a great deal of pressure on the couple. They must work together under very demanding circumstances. Many couples, especially those under twenty-five years of age, are likely to separate and divorce when they have young children.[37]

Reverting to Traditional Sex Roles

Upon the birth of the first child, couples tend to revert to extremely traditional sex roles.[38] A couple that made efforts to share tasks at home previously will find it particularly hard to keep this up. In many families, one person (usually the mother) stays home with the baby. She may also be responsible for almost all other household tasks and have few adult contacts. A middle-class mother living far from her family may be particularly isolated. Working-class and poor people are more likely to live closer to other relatives; often the women in these geographically and socially closer families help each other out. They are more likely than middle-class women to have one or two women in the family care for the children of other women who are employed or are otherwise unable to care for their children on a full-time basis. For example, working-class Italian Americans frequently live near their relatives, often in the same houses or streets. Household tasks and child care may be shared among the females. Meals are often shared by several families together. A tight network of aunts, uncles, cousins, and grandparents form a kind of social support system.[39] Black families, particularly poor ones or those in which the adults are marginally employed, also experience a kind of extended family network of sharing and helping. Often three or more generations of family will share a household. A grandmother or aunt may care for the children while the mother is working, going to school, or otherwise occupied.[40]

In middle-class and working-class families where the husband is employed, the husband is usually out of the house for most of the day. He is often tired when he arrives home from work and may be unable to give his wife the affection and help she needs. He may also feel somewhat incompetent at handling the baby because he has had little childhood preparation for this work and has not been developing his baby-care skills all day. In addition, he may feel that taking care of the baby is not "his job." Economic worries put added pressure on parents. If the mother is staying home with the baby, the family must rely totally on the income of the father. This may be particularly difficult to do because of high doctor and hospital bills for the baby's delivery and later care. The husband may thus feel doubly pressured to assume his "masculine" role of breadwinner.[41]

Many parents enjoy their infants and derive a great deal of satisfaction from their growing children. They feel that "having a family" is rewarding and brings the parents closer together. Research indicates that some life situations increase the likelihood of this actually happening while others decrease its chances. While the "Dick and Jane" readers tell us about the blissful life of the happy housewife and mother, studies show that as a group, full-time housewives are more prone to poor self-esteem, feelings of incompetence, alcoholism, drug abuse, marital dissatisfaction, and a variety of other difficulties than are mothers who work outside the home.[42] These problems are particularly characteristic of housewives who are dissatisfied with their lives.[43] In a study examining life satisfaction, 135 married working-class women with children were interviewed and asked how they spent their time and how happy they were. About half the women had jobs outside the home; the other half were full-time housewives. The wives who were employed reported that they were happier and more satisfied with their lives. They enjoyed their paychecks (and the social power and prestige they offered) and social contacts with customers and co-workers. The full-time housewives who described themselves as very happy were most likely to report as well a good deal of support from their close relationships with husbands and relatives.[44]

Judith Birnbaum studied three groups of middle-class women who had performed unusually well when they attended college fifteen to twenty-five years earlier: full-time homemakers with children, mothers who worked outside the home in professional jobs, and single, childless professional women. She found the full-time homemakers to have lower self-esteem and to be more insecure and unhappy than the other two groups of women. The full-time homemakers even described themselves as less competent at child care than did the mothers who worked outside the home. Full-time homemakers were more likely to describe having children as a "sacrifice," feeling them to be a duty and a responsibility, while the employed mothers were more likely to describe their children as providing enrichment and fulfillment.[45]

Other research indicates that women who work outside the home experience more equal power in the marital relationship compared to full-time housewives.[46] Employed women tend to have somewhat more influence in decision making in the family compared to housewives. Much of this power sharing is due to the increased economic power of these women. Although most men tend to "help out" with household tasks only minimally, some research suggests that they are slightly more likely to do so when the wife is employed full time.[47] This probably happens both because the woman has less time to do all the household tasks herself (someone has to get the work done) and because she has more power to request and get help from her husband compared to a full-time homemaker. There are, in addition, some husbands and wives who fully share household tasks when both work outside the home. Generally, they do this out of a commitment to an egalitarian relationship.

The overwhelming majority of wives and mothers who work outside the home are employed because they need the money. However, they also like the feeling of independence, competence, and involvement with others they usually receive on the job (even if the job is not such an interesting one).[48] The woman's paycheck also relieves men of some of the pressure to be the sole support of their families.

A popular myth is that children of employed women resent

not having a full-time homemaker-mother. One study found that
children are more or less accepting of their mothers' employment status depending on whether the job is viewed as an
economic necessity for family survival. Thus children of
working-class women were found to be more accepting of their
mothers' employment than middle-class children, who often did
not see a clear economic reason for the mothers' choice to act
outside the sex-role defined job of full-time homemaker.[49] A
number of studies have asked adolescents and young adults from
middle-class and working-class backgrounds to indicate whom
they would like to be like when they become adults. Many more
daughters of employed women chose their mothers as role
models, while daughters of homemakers were more likely to
choose people other than their mothers as models.[50] A woman
with greater variety and higher status in her life makes a more
attractive model with which her child can identify.

Mothers who work outside the home have their own
particular problems. A difficult or degrading job that offers little
satisfaction and creates anxiety over not being with children can
cause the employed mother to be quite unhappy; this unhappiness can have its effect on her children. Since the primary role of
caring for children is assigned to women, the lack of adequate
supports for working parents puts a special burden on the
mother.[51]

There are vast individual and some group differences in the
extent to which traditional sex roles are practiced and preached
within the two-parent heterosexual family. Some families make
a clear commitment to an egalitarian mode in which tasks,
power, and privilege are equally shared by adults, regardless of
sex. Building a truly egalitarian relationship is difficult, partly
because of societal limitations such as unequal employment and
income for men and women, lack of adequate part-time jobs for
parents, and lack of inexpensive and quality child-care facilities.
Couples who are committed to egalitarian relationships also
have to overcome cultural expectations and past socialization
for sex-role division of labor at home. A small but growing
number of couples are doing this.

In an analysis of sex-role stereotyping in white married
couples, Lillian Rubin points out the rarity of egalitarian-
ism among both middle-class and working-class couples.

However, in middle-class families an egalitarian *ideology* often exists, whereas working-class families more often consciously advocate traditional sex roles. Rubin found that in middle-class couples, women often have the freedom to develop their interests. She points out that this is necessary for the middle-class heterosexual man who often needs his wife to function as a charming hostess and companion to his business or professional colleagues. And since the middle-class man experiences more status, satisfaction, and power on his job than does the working-class man, he may be less in need of directly asserting his power and dominance over his wife and children. Among working-class people, there is little carryover from work to home; the wife does not entertain business colleagues. The sex-role divisions between men and women are more clearly defined and overtly practiced.[52]

Parenting Outside of the Nuclear Family

A growing number of people do not bring up children in two-parent, mother-father (also known as nuclear) families. Single mothers and fathers may have the full responsibility to care for the emotional and financial needs of their children. In most cases, it is the mother who is left with this responsibility, and usually she must work outside the home and rear her children. Unless they get a great deal of cooperation from family and friends, single parents may lead difficult lives. Potential lovers and friends may be reluctant to establish relationships with single parents for fear of having to share their parenting roles. In some ways the lot of the unmarried or divorced mother is worse than that of the widowed father or mother. She is often blamed by society either for having a child out of marriage or for not being able to hold her family together, since most people still consider it a woman's responsibility to keep her family "intact."

Because women are generally paid less for their employment, single mothers (most of whom receive little or no money for child support from their children's fathers) usually raise their children on a meager income. Many single mothers believe, however, that they and their children are better off in a loving, if struggling, household than in the basically unhappy ones they lived in before. Many other single mothers have always been single and have raised their children themselves as a matter of choice or circumstance. Recently a number of support groups for single mothers have been established, such as the Sisterhood of Black Single Mothers and the Single Parent Project, both in New York City, and Parents Without Partners, a nationwide group. These organizations offer community, friendship, and shared resources to single parents.

Divorced fathers have distinct problems. The process of separating from a wife and children can be very painful to a man. Usually divorced fathers do not live with their children but may see them on weekends or vacations. Some divorced fathers see their children often, while others see them rarely, if ever. Many divorced fathers complain bitterly about their increasingly stilted relationships with their growing children. They may take their children places or buy them things, but usually their relationships are not as "natural" as they might be if they lived in the same household. Because most males have not been raised to express their innermost feelings, many divorced fathers find it hard to share love with their children in ways other than giving money and things. This can lead to a somewhat distant relationship. Sometimes a father will lose contact with his children altogether.[53]

An increasing number of divorced couples are seeking joint custody of their children. A joint-custody arrangement might, for example, include a child spending half the week with one parent and half the week with the other parent. This arrangement helps to make the child feel loved and wanted by both parents. It also allows the parents to maintain close relationships with their children while retaining some time and space for themselves. Joint custody does, however, require a great deal of cooperation between the divorced parents as well as proximity of both parents' homes and the financial resources to have dual sets of clothes, toys, furniture, and so forth.[54] Thus it is most often an option for middle-class or wealthy parents.

Some single men and women are now adopting children on their own. Heterosexual men and women who either choose not to live in a couple or cannot find a partner they want to live and raise a child with, may apply for adoption, or a single woman may become pregnant and have a baby.[55] A growing number of

ion—personal control and self-esteem).
 limited job opportunities, severe job
a very pessimistic view of life, some
their skills in any one area of work.
n and some women, the intention and
d develop job skills.

ocialized to think about employment in
hood to males means putting aside
y and taking up a toolbox or finishing up
on professional life. Young men from
milies may see joining the armed forces
 job training or employment they are
n life. This may be especially true for
inorities who have fewer job opportun-
some women volunteer for the armed
nd military service is clearly more in
onal male role.

the main measure of social success. It is
oing socialization experience in men's
en expect to work an average of forty
weeks every year, every year between
ixty-fifth birthdays. (A more highly
ct to begin work a bit later.) A full-time
e on the job than in any other single
or females, paid work is usually not
e's general definition or worth. Most
e that their employment is secondary.
es along, the stereotypical woman will
achine or cease her typing, go to her
dren, and live happily ever after. Most
lized to believe that paid employment
an appropriate husband comes along),
y be necessary for family "extras"), or,
redom. The differential socializing of
males for family responsibilities is one
ities between women and men.

en working outside the home vary,
 or ethnic background. Young black
 to prepare to support themselves
eir white counterparts. In interview-

gay men and lesbians are also adopting children, although this is done without making sexual preferences known. In some states, such as New Jersey, there are policies assigning gay youths to lesbian foster homes. Some lesbians are choosing to become pregnant (either via sexual relations with men or by artifical insemination).[56]

The proportion of single parents and divorced parents living with new partners who are lesbian mothers or gay fathers is not known. However, their problems and experiences are similar, in many ways, to those of their heterosexual counterparts. Studies have found their children to be not remarkably different in adjustment from children of heterosexual single parents.[57] This is particularly true if the parent is publicly homosexual and self-accepting. [58] The majority of lesbian mothers and a minority of male gay fathers have children who are aware of their parents' sexual preferences: most children accept or seem to have no reaction to this information.[59] A study of homosexual fathers indicates that gay men are much happier with themselves as fathers, workers, and people if they have fully accepted their homosexuality and have been public about their preferences. This study found that "closeted gays," especially those remaining in heterosexual marriages, experienced the most conflict with their families. The publicly gay fathers were surprised to find a great deal more acceptance and positive regard than they had imagined from their children and their own parents, as well as from friends and co-workers. Publicly gay fathers' problems with child rearing do not appear to be greater than those of heterosexual single fathers.[60]

Many children of lesbians (and occasionally of gay males) share an important child-parent relationship with the parent's lover. These relationships are often caring, responsible, and important to both the child and the adult. Unfortunately, no research has yet been completed which fully explores the quality or the quantity of these relationships. Because these adults are not legal guardians of the children, they suffer a lack of parental rights. In addition, they are often not socially recognized as parents. While children generally accept their lesbian or gay male parents and their parents' lovers, there is no indication, at least from anecdotal accounts, that this will influence their future sexual preferences.

The lesbian couple often fears that children could be taken away by an angry ex-spouse or a biased social service agency. Family courts have taken custody of children away from capable lesbian mothers and awarded it to fathers, aunts, uncles, or grandparents. In some cases, foster care was preferred by the court. A recent survey of custody cases found that lesbian mothers who were open about their sexual preferences won custody of their own children in only 2 percent of the cases brought to court. Most custody cases never get to court because they require a great deal of money for legal fees and great risk on the part of the lesbian mother.[61]

Some gay parents stay in their heterosexual marriages while their children are growing up. Mothers and fathers sometimes make this choice because they believe it will be better for the children. Some lesbian mothers stay in their marriages for financial reasons. Fear of poverty and/or of socially unacceptable child-rearing conditions keep many gay fathers and mothers leading double lives, at least until their children are grown.

Some adults—both heterosexual and homosexual—choose to raise their children in communes or cooperatives. In these "extended" families, biologically unrelated adults, both single people and couples with or without children, live together and share child rearing, household tasks, and expenses. Commune members choose each other to live with and often have formal rules for functioning as well as schedules for sharing the work to be done. This system is economical in terms of both time and money, and it can offer the loving support of close friends on a daily basis. Commune children have the benefits of a number of adults and children to share close personal relationships with. Communes, like all family forms, often have difficulty over time. This may be due to the shifting plans of each member and to the fact that few of us are raised or prepared to live in a sharing household with a large number of people. Some adults appreciate the benefits of a commune or extended family, but also want more personal privacy.[62] They have created cooperatives in which some tasks, such as child care or cooking, are shared but in which each member or family lives in their own separate apartment or home.

The nontraditional family formulations described above do not always minimize or eliminate sex roles. Members of

ingredients of satisfac
Due to poor training
discrimination, and/or
people never develop
However, for most me
reality is to settle in a

Men and women are
different ways. Adult
fantasies of football glo
in school and starting
working-class or poor f
as a way of gaining th
unable to find in civili
blacks and other racial
ities in general. While
forces, more men do, a
keeping with the traditi

Paid work, for men, is
the most important ong
lives. After all, most m
hours every week, fifty
their eighteenth and
educated man would exp
worker spends more tim
activity in a lifetime. F
considered central to o
girls are trained to belie
When the right man com
allegedly put down her
beautiful home, have chi
female children are socia
is either temporary (until
occasional (as money ma
perhaps for relief from bo
males for paid work and fe
root of the social inequal

Attitudes toward wom
depending on one's racia
women are more likely
economically than are th

ing young black women, Joyce Ladner found that they do not expect to be supported by men and do expect to have to provide for their families themselves.[65] Other ethnic groups also carry some historical and cultural baggage that affects, among other things, their attitudes toward work.[66]

Members of different social classes also have differing views of women's paid employment.[67] Although a working-class couple may need a second income, working-class women are generally paid less for more boring jobs than are middle-class women. So the option of working outside the home may seem less attractive to the young working-class woman than to the middle-class young woman. Since working-class couples are more likely to retain a traditionally sex-role-defined life-style, women and men may feel strongly that the woman should stay at home. In working-class families in which both parents are employed, the economic need for the woman's employment is more evident. This economic need may make the man feel particularly aware that his income alone is insufficient to keep his family afloat. He may feel that having an employed wife symbolizes that he is not adequately fulfilling his "masculine" role of breadwinner.

Contrary to the myth, however, the reality is that most women are gainfully employed. The statistics on how many women work for pay vary, depending on the source. For example, the U.S. Department of Labor offers statistics only on regularly employed, tax-paying workers. Their figures do not include the millions of people who work on an "off-the-books" basis, which includes many types of work done in the home (baby-sitting, for example) or some part-time work (such as bookkeeping). These types of jobs are more likely to be held by women because they are more complementary to the roles of child rearer and homemaker. These jobs may have shorter and more flexible hours, and are more clearly defined as "women's work"—work that fits within our society's stereotype of what women are supposed to be good at. These jobs usually pay the least, often below the legally allowed minimum wage. But if a woman sees her main job as child rearer and homemaker, she is not as likely to complain if she gets paid less. She may feel fortunate to have some work that doesn't interfere too much with her other responsibilities. Thus, official government statistics must be understood with these limitations in mind.

The Department of Labor reports that approximately 40 percent of the total official American work force is female. In the last two decades, female employment has grown at a much faster rate than has male employment. Now about half of all women and three quarters of all men over sixteen years of age are employed. Although a large number of women who work are single, separated, divorced, or widowed, the majority of women workers are married.[68] Most wives who work do so on a full-time basis. According to government statistics, over half of all married women with children between the ages of six and seventeen are employed, and about one third of those with children under six years work for pay.[69] In a more in-depth analysis of varieties of work-force participation, over 60 percent of all American women were found to be employed on some level within six months of the birth of their first child.[70] Clearly most women are and will be employed, whether or not they are fully prepared for it.

When women enter the labor market they experience it differently than do men. Women get less money for their work than men: working women earn 59 percent of what working men earn annually. The difference between men's and women's income has actually *increased* in the last fifteen years.[71] Recently, the director of the Women's Bureau of the Department of Labor reported that the average female college graduate earns about the same as the average male high school graduate and the average female high school graduate earns about the same as the average male with an eighth-grade education.[72]

While there has been a great deal of publicity about women taking over "men's jobs," in reality women and men are usually segregated into different jobs with different job titles. There are some industries or jobs which are dominated by women employees. The percentage of female workers in typical occupations is: registered nurses, 97 percent; elementary school teachers, 85 percent; typists, 96 percent; telephone operators, 93 percent; secretaries, 99 percent; hairdressers, 90 percent; waiters and waitresses, 91 percent; nursery aides, 85 percent; sewers and stitchers, 95 percent; private household workers, 97 percent; cashiers, 88 percent; bank tellers, 92 percent; and payroll clerks, 77 percent.[73] According to a special task force report to the Secretary of Health, Education and Welfare, women's occupations are closely related either to their role of homemaker (as in the case of teachers, nurses or aides, hairdressers, waitresses, seamstresses, household workers) or to their role as helpmate to men (as in the case of secretaries, typists, cashiers, bank tellers, payroll clerks).[74] In contrast, men's jobs usually involve working with large machines, doing technical procedures, agricultural labor, construction, mining, managerial work, and work in the professions (not including teaching, nursing, or social work).[75] The jobs most available to women are usually lower in status, pay, and promotion possibilities than those available to men. Fewer women are in unionized jobs, which means that they have less job security and fewer rights on the job—in general, less of the benefits that are negotiated on a collective basis.[76]

A similar discrepancy exists between whites and blacks. Blacks earn significantly less than whites; in 1977, the median income for black families was $9,562 compared to $16,740 for white families. In addition, many jobs are segregated by race as well as by sex, though this practice, like sex-segregation, is illegal.

The fact that men have relatively "better" jobs than women does not mean that either are terribly satisfied with their employment situations; most people are not.[77] For men there is no other socially acceptable choice: they must work or be seen as failures as men. For women, the option of not working (though often mythical) can further limit them in trying to get good jobs. Although today most women work for pay, most of their mothers did not. Due to discrimination and poor training, few women have managed to get and keep high-status, high-paying jobs. Thus, most women lack role models in the labor force. It is difficult for a woman to forge ahead into a male-dominated job, to return to school for further training in a supposedly "masculine" field, or to be the supervisor of women and men. She needs to be a pioneer. Studies show that women whose mothers worked when they were growing up are more able to handle the stresses of a high-pressure, traditionally masculine field.[78] Some women fear they will not be attractive to men if their job status or pay is too high or if they are engaged in traditionally masculine work.[79]

Many women are the sole supports of their families and must work to survive. Yet many employers use some sex-stereotypical excuses for not hiring or promoting women. Some say that men and women alike do not like to be supervised by a woman. Supervising and being feminine are antithetical in our culture. Therefore, most women bosses are seen as socially unacceptable. Many employers keep women out of desirable positions because they feel that women are likely to opt for the home and family and leave their jobs more often than men. Statistically this is only partially true. If a woman has a boring and low-paying job and no access to inexpensive and adequate child care, she may not be eager—or able—to return to her old job once she has a child. However, if a woman finds her job worth returning to, she is very likely to do so even when her baby is quite young. One study found that the difference between male and female incomes was due primarily to discrimination in hiring, training, and promotion and not to breaks in work due to job changes, children, illness, or absence.[80]

Women are excluded from certain high-paying but dangerous jobs. Some employers do this out of respect for what they see as "femininity." Some do it to avoid potential lawsuits. Seven women filed suit against their employer, the American Cyanamid Co., for forcing them to have sterilization operations. The women were working in the plant's pigmentation department in which high levels of lead were used. The company feared that lead could damage a fetus being carried by one of their women workers and that this damage would leave them liable in a lawsuit. The company allegedly told the women that if they were not sterilized they would lose their $6.60-hourly wage jobs. In an area where few options for work exist (West Virginia), the majority of the women, almost all of whom were the sole or main supporters of their families, chose the operations. The remaining women were transferred to janitorial work at a lower wage or were laid off.[81]

Sex discrimination at the workplace reinforces traditional sex roles: men get better pay so they are more likely to keep working; women get poorer pay and lower-status jobs so they may opt for staying home to care for children. If parents have just so much money to spend on educating their children, the realities of the job scene may encourage mothers and fathers to spend it on their sons and not their daughters. Women sometimes do not take themselves as seriously on the job because they expect that they will be there on a temporary basis. On this, their employers usually concur. Women's sense of self is not as dependent on their jobs as is men's and they have the social, if not the economic, option of staying home and avoiding employment.

In young adulthood, people find that their early sex-role training often matches with the educational, marital, child-rearing, and economic demands of the world around them. Not surprisingly, the socialization process prepares young people to accept the world as it is. As the world is changing very quickly, however, for example with regard to the economic need for most women to work outside the home, that early sex-role training can create many conflicts for individuals. The conflicts may be especially intense during the young adult years when women and men are just beginning to take on adult responsibilities. Frequently, they are adjusting to the demands of marriage and parenthood as well as to new roles in the paid work force. As people move into middle adulthood, their older children may no longer demand so much attention and their work lives may be more settled. Although they have many responsibilities, adults may now be more likely to pause and consider the meaning of some of the traditionally masculine and traditionally feminine roles that they have taken on.

SIX:
Middle Adulthood

Reevaluating Life Choices

THE LONG PERIOD between about thirty-five to sixty years of age is typified by an increase in both power and responsibility.[1] Middle adults often take responsibility for their own aging

parents who may need physical, emotional, and/or financial support. For people who have been consistently employed, this is the period in which possible promotions and greater successes may mean increased work-related duties. With these enlarged responsibilities often comes an increase in power.

Middle adulthood is also the period in life in which one may try to make up for and do the things that were missing earlier on.[2] For those who have not had consistent and/or successful employment, this period is sometimes a time to try to develop new work skills and opportunities. During middle adulthood, parents, and mothers in particular, may have significantly more

freedom to explore their own interests now that their children are older and more independent.

In an extensive interview study, Bernice Neugarten found that most men define their position in the life cycle in terms of their paid work while women mark their position according to their families' growth and change.[3] For example, a man might mark the transition from young to middle adulthood by an important promotion, while a woman might indicate that she has made that transition once all her children are teenagers. In the latter part of middle adulthood, a shift in the social and emotional aspects of sex roles begins which is highly related to changes in the economic roles men and women are expected to play as they approach their sixties and seventies.

Job and Career Development

For many men, middle adulthood is marked by their becoming more highly skilled workers, getting the best shifts, getting better jobs or promotions, becoming foremen, having seniority and therefore more security on the job. By this time the male ethic of "word hard, get ahead" has paid off (though usually quite modestly). However, many working people, men as well as women, are not particularly satisfied with their jobs.[4] According to a study sponsored by *Playboy* magazine, which interviewed 1,990 American men between the ages of eighteen and forty-nine, one of the most important ways they felt deprived was in finding satisfaction in their work.[5] A large minority of people who are employed in interesting and rewarding work do derive satisfaction from their employment. In any case, more benefits on the job have been accrued by the individual who has been steadily employed throughout adulthood. If nothing else, at least most steadily employed workers can look forward to aging with some type of pension, meager though it may be. Workers who are marginally employed (working on and off or on a part-time basis) in low-status, low-paying jobs, may find themselves with few work-related rewards, financial or otherwise. Women are likely to be in these less desirable jobs.

During middle adulthood, approximately 55 percent of American women are employed.[6] However, they are less likely

than men to have high-status, adequately paying jobs. Before
they are thirty-five, many women have taken a leave of absence
from the paid work force, primarily for child-rearing purposes.
Rarely is a woman's job held open for her until she is ready to
return. She loses all her accumulated seniority. Often she is seen
as primarily committed to child care and therefore is offered less
responsible work. She is more heavily supervised and much
more poorly paid than her male age-mate. While the middle-
adult male may be reaping returns on his job, the middle-adult
female is often just beginning to strive for success in the world of
work.

In addition to these external barriers are internal ones. Many
women who spend several years as full-time homemakers find it
personally difficult to return to paid employment. Often they
feel as though their former competence had vanished. They may
be anxious about their ability to continue their domestic tasks.
They may receive little support from children and husbands
who have learned to depend on them to do all domestic chores.
While some families are quite helpful when the mother returns
to paid work, others sabotage her efforts by increasing their
demands on her and making her feel guilty about "abandoning"
the family. She may feel she has to work doubly hard, both at
work and at home, to prove she is both a good worker and a good
wife and mother. Again, she must deal with her personal
ambivalence as well as her lack of opportunity. Yet most women
do overcome these obstacles and get what is to be gotten out of
their jobs.

In an in-depth interview study of white mid-life women,
Lillian Rubin found important social-class differences in
women's feelings about returning to paid employment. When
economic necessity was not a factor, women felt great ambivalence about working outside the home. This often translated
into immobility and indecision. Working-class women were no
more or less eager to return to work, but did so with less
ambivalence in order to help support their families. Although
working-class husbands did not like the fact that their own
paychecks were insufficient to support the family, economic
need often resulted in a shift in attitudes toward women's
employment. Many working-class couples viewed the wife's
employment as a temporary matter to help during a period of

economic stress; in fact, the money problems never seemed to end. Rubin found that the middle-class women were more likely to experience guilt due to their husband's insistence that they should work only if they really wanted to. Because the society makes women feel that their primary role is wife and mother, the *choice* to work is often fraught with great ambivalence. This pattern of guilt among middle-class women fits with Rubin's earlier study which found that children were more accepting of their mothers' employment if they felt it was an economic necessity. For most of the women Rubin interviewed (both working-class and middle-class), approval from the husband was a necessary ingredient in order for them to make commitments to activities outside of the home, including employment and education.[7]

In recent years, many mid-life women have returned to school for further training. They may enter high school equivalency programs, trade schools, colleges, and graduate schools.[8] There is evidence that women in middle adulthood do not suffer from the same motivational barriers to achievement as do younger women. Rhoda Baruch found that during this period, women often experience a great surge of achievement motivation and have increased hopes of developing themselves for interesting and rewarding jobs.[9] Having settled the issue of their feminine identity through the choice of a clear life-style (either through the traditional route of marriage and motherhood or by establishing clear alternative life styles), most women in middle adulthood are more assertive and less sentimental than they were when they were younger.[10] These factors, plus their adult experiences, often make middle-adult women excellent students. But these newly assertive and committed women are sometimes greeted with a skeptical welcome, especially in institutions of higher learning. Inadequate child-care facilities (including after-school programs) may keep some women from returning to school. Part-time students, particularly in graduate school, are sometimes not taken seriously by their professors.[11] Many colleges and universities now have programs to facilitate the reentry of women returning to college and graduate school.[12]

Despite many demands on women, middle adulthood often offers them the chance to expand and grow and to experience the pleasure of successful approaches to new goals. However, because society claims women's primary responsibility is as mother and wife, many women who experience success in their employment or volunteer work do not fully incorporate these aspects of themselves into their own self-definitions. A large number of employed women Lillian Rubin interviewed did not mention their jobs in response to a question asking them to describe who and what they were. These women were most likely to see the active, intellectual, work-professional sides of their personalities as divorced from the core self—which they described as more passive, emotional, and dependent. Rubin interprets this desire to split two essential aspects of self as an outgrowth of previously contradictory socialization experiences: encouragement to be bright but not too bright as to outdo men, to be friendly but not too aggressive. Because most people are apt to see a married woman as an extension of her husband, even the woman who does manage to blend major commitments both in and out of the family often acquiesces in the social stereotype. She may thus claim a divided self-image, one that often denies the strength and importance of her less traditional dimensions.[13]

For men, several problems related to traditional sex roles are likely to occur in mid-life. During a period of life in which one is supposed to wield power and prestige, the man who does not may feel as though he has failed. If he has not made his mark at work, he may feel as though his male identity is being questioned. He may feel inadequate if he is unable to provide full financial support for his children or his parents. Involvement with family may be one of the few potential sources of satisfaction available to him, yet his sense of self-defeat may keep him away. This is particularly true for the man who is frequently unemployed. In a nation which almost always has a large portion (5 to 10 percent) of its active work force unemployed and a much larger portion underemployed, a substantial number of men view their own work records as proof of their failure as men.

At the other extreme, the superachieving man who has made it in the world of work may also, at this stage of life, stop and say, "Where has this gotten me?" Daniel Levinson calls this the "mid-life transition" whereby the man reevaluates his life and begins doing things he wants to do but didn't do earlier.[14] The successful stereotypic man may bring home a good paycheck and may even enjoy his work. As he examines his life, however, he decides he wants to pursue more personally or socially meaningful endeavors. Yet he is at somewhat of a loss to do so. Like his female counterpart struggling to reenter the work force, the middle-adult man may be struggling to reenter the close bonds of family and friends. He may be awkward in approaching his children whom he may have previously excluded. His prior focus on work often teaches his loved ones that he is not available and that he is not to be depended upon for emotional needs. His children may go to their mother with their problems. They may see their father as the judgmental family figurehead who should not be disturbed.[15] The man who wants to break out of this mold may not know how to. He may have few resources from childhood training and few role models to help him.

Personal Relationships

As mid-life women and men reevaluate their family and work lives, changes in the marital relationship may occur. Often more egalitarian modes develop during this period. A wife's employment enhances her power in family decison making. Especially in middle-class couples, a somewhat greater sharing of roles now takes place. Men may become more interested in their children or may take up gourmet cooking. Women may be returning to school or employment and may gain authority and esteem in their family's eyes. The sense of marital satisfaction, however, will still depend greatly upon the level of self-satisfaction. Thus people who feel fairly dissatisfied with their own lives will continue to feel more negatively about their families and their partners and may be resistant to change. Those who feel good about themselves will be more likely to enjoy their families and partners and be flexible about change. For those who are parents, the shift in family roles during middle adulthood is quite marked. The children are growing up, becoming more independent, and leaving home. By the time the average woman and man are in their early fifties, their last child has been married.[16] They usually have fifteen to twenty years ahead of them before retirement.

For almost all women who primarily devoted themselves to the care of their children and husbands, this shift in the family is usually seen as both exciting and frightening. Lillian Rubin found that most women are delighted to see their children grow up and leave the home, and to have the opportunity to develop their own new identities. They are pleased not to have to give so much of themselves to their families' demands and needs. Says a forty-two-year-old mother of two, "I'm ready to feel some freedom; I'm just itching for it. I'm looking forward, finally, to having a life of my own again. It's been such a long time."[17]

Now the mid-life woman can decide what she wants to do for the years to come depending on her own needs and interests. For many, the choice to seek employment and/or further education is part of that decision. For some, the ambivalence of this new-found freedom is quite difficult to handle. A fifty-one-year-old homemaker describes herself as follows: "I'm Dennis and Derek Clark's mother, and Mike Clark's wife. That's who I am, right there. After that, I'm just a blank. I don't know if I'm anything else; it's been so many years."[18] For the woman who fears she is not competent except as a mother and wife, the future can be very threatening. The extent to which a mid-life woman has had varied sources of self-definition, interests, and involvement, and the extent to which she receives support for her greater desire to reach out and grow, will greatly determine the quality of this mid-life transition. According to Rubin, the question women didn't ask at adolescence, "What am I going to do with the rest of my life?" returns to haunt them at mid-life.[19]

Interestingly enough, Rubin found that men were more likely than women to be extremely upset by their children growing up and leaving the home. The women she interviewed believed they had participated in each step of their children's development and were basically ready for separation from them. But their husbands felt that the years had slipped by without their really getting to know their children. The man in his middle years may be more open to closeness with family than ever before. But that family is now about to disperse. Many fathers want to hold on to their children at this point. The timing of the mid-life man's needs is not "in synch" with that of his newly independent family members.

During middle adulthood, married couples are no longer bound together by their children. Many women report feeling more satisfied with their marriages once the children leave home.[20] For others, divorces occur during this period. Some couples work out their problems within their marriages. The majority of middle-aged women in Rubin's study complained about what they perceived to be a lack of communication, understanding, and respect for their individual needs on the part of their husbands. The husbands frequently complained about and felt uncomfortable with their wives' constant demands for personal discussion and emotional expression. These differences in expectations and needs, differences that are highly related to earlier socialization, may function to keep women and men apart. They may make it more difficult for women and men to have truly loving, mutual relationships.

Many men go through a type of "mid-life crisis" largely out of a fear of aging and of life passing them by; this crisis can sometimes end in divorce.[21] The divorced man faces being single somewhat differently from his female counterpart. The availability and social acceptability of liaisons with younger women allow mid-life men to date and find new partners more readily than do females. For men, age, and the power and financial security that may come with it, is compatible with (and may even enhance) attractiveness. This is not the case for women. Often the personal crisis of the man is temporarily patched up, though not resolved, by a new relationship that still carries the old marks of emotional dependency and an inability to communicate. The mid-life man is unlikely to find real satisfaction simply by shifting partners. More significant personal change may be necessary for that to be accomplished. The divorced mid-life woman, in addition to being considered less attractive than a man of her age, may well be unemployed and without job skills. And as a woman, she may face severe job discrimination. She is less likely to remarry than the divorced mid-life man. So the divorced woman often is faced with adjusting to poverty and to living alone. For divorced men and women who do not remarry immediately, being single sometimes allows them the opportunity to better understand themselves and their own needs and interests.

For mid-life adults who are likely to be going through major transitions, friends may be particularly important. Friends sometimes share similar experiences and may assure one another of the "normality" of their lives. They can offer a steady source of support, companionship, and affection. A peer relationship also provides an arena in which equality and personal respect are common and usually consistent. Because of their early sex-role training, women are more likely than men to have established close friendships where feelings and problems are discussed.

For people who live alone, friends may be even more central, and single people may have more time and emotional energy than people in couples do to build meaningful relationships with friends. The personal independence that may come with being single sometimes allows the individual to be particularly selective about friends and activities.[22] In the last decade a new consciousness about being single has arisen; there is more social support for living alone. Younger single people are now more likely to have positively and consciously chosen their way of life. People who are now in middle adulthood did not grow up with the advantage of this new consciousness. It will be interesting to see how single people in the next generation fare as they go through the life cycle with a new appreciation and respect for their single status.

Changes in Sexuality

Toward the end of middle adulthood, almost all women and men experience changes in their sexuality which can be fairly startling or disturbing. Women begin to go through menopause usually between forty-eight and fifty-five years of age. Menopause marks the end of ovulation, menstruation, and the ability to reproduce. This means fewer worries about birth control and pregnancy. But it is also interpreted by our culture as marking the end of youthful sexuality. Some women feel "desexed" or "neutered" by menopause. Other women do not. When the body lowers its production of estrogen and progesterone, some women experience mood swings, which can be frightening. Most women, however, do not suffer from these mood swings. Myths about women going through menopause encourage people to believe that an older woman is no longer sexual and makes the sexual postmenopausal woman feel abnormal and "oversexed." In reality, her sexuality is healthy and can be a source of pleasure for her for many years to come. Clinical studies show that menopause does not negatively affect sexual pleasure or performance.[23] In fact, women with positive self-images and loving partners often find this time of their lives very exciting sexually. They have the experience to know what pleases them and their partners, they are capable of multiple orgasms, and they can sustain sexual involvement and interest for a long period of time. In addition, because of physiological changes which create a more complex and extensive system of veins in the genital area, women increase their sexual capacities with age.[24] A number of studies indicate that sexual pleasure for women tends to increase with age and length of relationship with the current partner.[25] In a questionnaire study of 3,000 women from fourteen to seventy-eight years of age, Shere Hite asked women to explain how age had affected sex for them. The vast majority of women felt their sexual pleasure increased with age. One woman said: "I am enjoying sex more in my forties than I did in my thirties; I enjoyed it more in my thirties than in my twenties. There's a liberating combination of experience, self-knowledge, and an absence of pregnancy fears."[26]

Given our culture's views on youthful feminine beauty, many women approaching later adulthood feel unattractive and unlovable. This may be particularly true for unusually attractive women for whom socially defined beauty was a major source of positive identity.[27] Middle adulthood is a time when women who have the money may go off to health and beauty spas. Cosmetic surgery is not uncommon among wealthy women who are in their fifties or older. Most people, however, do not have the money for such measures. But many of the feelings and attitudes toward the progressively aging woman cross over class, ethnic, and racial group lines. Sometimes the woman approaching later adulthood fears she has little to offer a partner by way of sexual attractiveness. Thus she believes her value as a woman is greatly diminished. A woman may fear that her mate will abandon her for a younger, seemingly more attractive women. Women who are not in long-term relationships may fear that they will no longer be able to get partners because of their progressive aging.

Those who have a multiplicity of interests, talents, and attractions, or who reject the Madison Avenue-Hollywood version of beauty and sexuality, are less likely to feel anxiety about their sexual attractiveness.

Because much of the lesbian community is acutely aware of the negative aspects of "sexploitation," the aging process may be less threatening to their sexuality. Some women who had heterosexual relationships during adolescence and young adulthood may develop lesbian sexual preferences during middle adulthood. For some, the special emotional closeness shared between women grows into a sexual relationship as well. It is hard to say whether these shifts are developmental trends that have occurred frequently in the past and will continue in the future. It is possible that women who in the past felt socially pressured into entering traditionally heterosexual relationships now have more support to assert themselves as lesbians.[28]

Males also go through shifts in their sexual functioning at the end of middle adulthood, and some researchers believe that there is a male menopause.[29] The production of sperm decreases during this period, although some sperm production continues until death. There is a clear decrease in strength and stamina, both cornerstones of the masculine sexual ideal. Older men can achieve orgasm, but they are slower to arouse and require more stimulation than they did when they were younger. Many men experience occasional impotence (the inability to sustain an erection). This can be very anxiety-provoking to a man and his partner. Often it can spiral into generalized anxiety about and then avoidance of sexual involvement. Contrary to social stereotypes, Bernice Neugarten and her colleagues found that middle-aged men were more concerned about physical attractiveness and deterioration of their bodies than were middle-aged women.[30]

During middle adulthood many men with homosexual preferences experience shifts in their sexual functioning and self-images as well. For the long-time gay man, self-acceptance and appreciation are common during this period. For men who previously hid or denied their sexual preferences, middle adulthood may be the time to "come out." Some men who had sporadic homosexual relationships earlier on, but who were in heterosexual marriages, may establish more exclusively gay relationships. The recent gay rights movement has supported men in their desire to come out as homosexuals. However, the mainstream subculture of the male gay community, which is predominently white and middle class, tends to emphasize youth and beauty for its participants. Thus the middle-adult gay man may face some of the same anxieties and difficulties as do heterosexual women in attracting and keeping sexual partners.[31]

Sex differences in socialization patterns can create a number of ongoing problems in the sexual relationships of many heterosexual men and women. For most women, sex is seen as embedded in the context of a relationship. During their formative years, females are taught that "good girls" have sex with husbands who love them deeply and forever. Any other kind of sexual involvement is seen as demeaning. Thus, the quality and quantity of sexual involvement may depend on how close the woman feels emotionally to her lover. For most men, sex and emotions are not so thoroughly intertwined. And many men feel uncomfortable expressing affection for their partners in any way other than through sexual relations. The result is a mismatch: she wants to talk, to share feelings and then sex; he wants to have sex. Their agendas for lovemaking are different because their upbringing on this important aspect of life—sexuality—has been different.

Another somewhat ironic mismatch for heterosexual men and women is their shifting interest in sexual involvement during middle adulthood. Many women's sexual interest begins to soar as they have fewer responsibilities to young children and no longer worry about pregnancy. Many, for the first time in their lives, begin to initiate sexual activity with their husbands. For many men, this new sexual assertiveness is inconsistent with their well-socialized image of sexually passive women. The woman's newfound independence and self-definition are likely to energize her and give her greater sexual interests and appetites at the same time that the man's sense of impending decline makes him less interested in and perhaps fearful of sex.

Power struggles and general problems within a particular relationship may get played out within the sexual arena.[32]

Sexuality for single adults, as compared to people in couples, more often includes relationships with a number of different people over a period of time. Many single people have a series of monogamous relationships which are close and quite satisfying. Many do not. Anxieties about changes in sexual functioning and attractiveness are similar for the single and coupled adult. One drawback for single people adapting to mid-life changes in sexuality is that they are less likely than adults in couples to have a strong and reliable relationship with a sexual partner. On the other hand, the single individual may be less fearful of being abandoned because she or he has already adapted to a single life-style.

The last ten to fifteen years have brought a significantly more open and accepting attitude toward sexuality for men and women. While this has helped to liberate people from many of their fears about sex, it has also created some problems as well. Those mid-life adults who were socialized to express their sexual needs in an extremely restrictive and repressed fashion may feel negatively about themselves when they are confronted by new sexual norms, not only by their partners, but by the media as well. A sexually permissive atmosphere can place undue demands for performance on both men and women. Many adults who cannot meet a fantasized but highly publicized version of sexual prowess may feel inadequate, as may adolescents and adults at every age. A solid self-image and supportive partner or partners may help both women and men to resist the pressure that may be created by these new sexual "ideals."[33]

SEVEN:
Later Adulthood

The Diminishing Importance of Sex Roles

AS PEOPLE MOVE INTO THEIR SIXTIES, they tend to become less stereotypically feminine or masculine. This happens within all social classes. As men age, they tend to see themselves as giving

and needing to receive more nurturance than ever before. Older women tend to be more assertive and self-oriented.[1] The changes in the structure of both women's and men's lives during the later adulthood period encourage a more androgynous approach to sex roles.

As in other periods of development, age and stage are not necessarily identical. This is particularly true during later adulthood, when one's health and vigor are better determinants of "aging" than simple chronological age. An active and healthy seventy-eight-year-old will have different developmental problems and goals than a seventy-eight-year-old invalid.

The Quality of Life

A large number of old people live in poverty. While most people work hard all of their lives, about sixteen percent of all people over sixty-five live in impoverished circumstances. The statistics on black people are even more distressing: 36 percent of elderly blacks live below the poverty level. White retired workers live quite modestly on an average of $210 per month from Social Security plus whatever pensions they may have. Black retired workers average $168 monthly from Social Security. Their previously lower-paying jobs leave blacks with scantier savings, pensions, and Social Security benefits in old age.[2]

Even for older people who do not officially qualify as "poor," life is often an economic struggle. In the United States, there are approximately 22 million Americans over age sixty-five. The average annual family income for elderly whites is $7,519 and for elderly blacks it is $4,909.[3] For most elderly people, severe economic conditions mean a life of scrimping, very careful buying, cutting back on almost all luxuries, and remaining in old and often deteriorated neighborhoods. About 60 percent of the aged live in and around cities. Eighty percent of men over sixty-five years of age live with their wives, while only 50 percent of women over sixty-five live with husbands. This is due to greater longevity of women and a cultural trend for females to marry somewhat older males. About 9 percent of all the elderly live with younger family members; among blacks, 28 percent live with younger people—primarily family. This difference may partly be due to a tradition of pooling resources among blacks.[4] Contrary to some media images of old people spending their lives in nursing homes, in reality only 5 percent of the elderly are institutionalized, although about 86 percent of them have chronic health problems.[5]

Some older people are seeking out new living situations to suit their current needs. A significant number of elderly men and women are living together outside the confines of marriage. These relationships usually are quite similar to those of their married peers. Seniors often avoid marriage because it would require the woman (often a widow) to give up her former husband's Social Security, making it much more difficult to survive. The fact that many older people are living together outside of marriage speaks to the generally altered view of at least the formal aspects of the institution. In a significant way, it is a testimony to the diminishing importance of the sexual double standard.

A second new living arrangement is communal living. For older people with limited resources and a great need for social connection and involvement, communal living may be a viable alternative. At present, a relatively small number of elderly people live communally; they must be willing to give up some privacy and some tradition. One such commune of older people is housed in a renovated town house in Chicago. Twelve people (the youngest of whom is sixty-nine years of age) share their expenses, their household duties, and a good part of their emotional lives.[6]

Another new trend for older adults is living in retirement communities. Over a half million Americans live in such communities. Often these consist of cooperative or condominium housing units inhabited by relatively affluent women and men. Retirement communities generally feature expensive and extensive recreational and cultural facilities. While these communities can offer some elderly people an active recreational and social life, they have the marked disadvantage of isolating older people from the rest of the community. For the healthy and wealthy individual who has enough mobility to get out of the retirement community frequently, this kind of living may be very satisfying. But for older people who are either ill or who have limited financial resources, the retirement community can be very confining.[7]

Illness and impending death are perhaps the most difficult features of aging. While a good deal of research has been done on people's attitudes toward these events,[8] little of it has analyzed sex differences in attitudes. One would suspect, however, that traditional sex-role definitions affect men's and women's respective reactions to illness and death. The incompatability of illness, debilitation, and dependency with the traditional masculine ideal is obvious. Does this contribute to a more difficult acceptance of old age for men than for women? Does it possibly add to lower life expectancy for men than for women? How does a woman whose feminine self-image has revolved around nurturing others adapt to invalidism and a life of needing the help of others? Undoubtedly the way one deals with illness and dying reflects many dimensions of one's personality; sex roles is sure to be one of them.

Retirement

Most people retire by age sixty-five or seventy: most are forced to; many choose to. Retirement generally means a radical change in social and financial status and in daily activity. For some adults, it is a pleasure not to have to go to work; other interests take employment's place and economic security prevents serious financial problems. For others, retiring from work seems to mean retiring from life. This is particularly true of people who have had little of meaning in their lives except for work.[9] Due to traditional sex-role prescriptions, this is significantly more common for men than for women. The end of work means the end of the traditional measure of male achievement and value; for some men it symbolizes a loss of masculinity. This is the stage in life when men who accepted extreme versions of the masculine ideal may suffer greatly. Those whose lives and values were more diverse have fewer adjustment problems. Since women are generally not defined primarily by their achievements on the job, retirement is usually less traumatic for them than for men. This does not mean, however, that work is not important to women. A recent study found that at age seventy, women were most satisfied if they had led work-centered or group-centered lives, rather than family-centered lives.[10] Given traditional sex roles, when women work outside the home they continue to have other interests and activities (such as close family ties, friendships, and homemaking tasks).

After retirement, husbands and wives whose daily lives were strictly separated by different work places now find themselves face to face, not only with no children but with open schedules. They spend much more time together than ever before and they may have fewer social supports and opportunities for separate activities. In an interview study, Alan Kerckhoff found that most husbands look forward to the end of paid work, while wives may be ambivalent about their husbands' retirement. Women who define themselves as housekeepers tend to feel much more negative about their husbands' retirement than do women who define themselves as primarily giving affection to and caring for their husbands.[11] Some women who have been full-time homemakers or who have been fully in charge of the kitchen and general housework may find their "helping" husbands a nuisance. They may carefully guard their domestic dominance and fear their husband's takeover. A couple that has consistently shared some household tasks may find the retired husband's greater involvement in domestic work consistent and pleasurable. In many cases, the absence of the usually superior status and economic resources of the man over the woman also serves to make decision making and power division more egalitarian among older couples.

Depression, even leading to suicide, is not uncommon for the elderly, particularly among white males. Some researchers in the field of aging believe that retirement and physical decline are particularly hard for white men to adjust to because of their previously high status.[12] Aging and the progressive inability to match up to the ideal masculine standard can be quite depressing for some men.

Longevity and Family Roles

The life expectancy of women is significantly greater than that of men. The average white woman can expect to live seventy-six and a half years; the average black woman, seventy-one years. The average white man lives until age sixty-nine while the average black man lives to age sixty-three. Most researchers agree that physiological differences (such as lower female cholesterol levels) as well as social and psychological factors explain women's higher life expectancy. These social and psychological differences include the high pressure of the male role, with its emphasis on achievement; the lack of emotional release experienced by most men; and the greater physical dangers of many jobs held by men and denied to women. Men more than women suffer from severe heart conditions, high blood pressure, strokes, gastrointestinal disease, and cancer. The poor longevity of black people is also attributed to more heavy physical and dangerous work, poorer health-care services, and a greater incidence of high blood pressure, strokes, and diabetes.[13]

Because of this major difference in life expectancy and the social practice of pairing a somewhat older male with a younger female, many older women are widows. Over 85 percent of all widowed people are women. Over half of all women over sixty-five years of age are widows, and they are likely to live another fifteen years as widows.[14]

After a period of mourning for the lost spouse, most people set out to adjust and form new lives for themselves. Most widowed men remarry as soon as it is feasible. They seem to want the companionship and nurturance of marriage. Men tend to enjoy the institution of marriage and thus seek it out in older age. Those older men who do not remarry tend not to make other ongoing social contacts and are fairly lonely. Women, on the other hand, do not usually seek out remarriage after they have been widowed. Rather, they are likely to seek out the companionship of other women. Most older women, in contrast to older men, have one or more confidantes and, usually, a network of friends. They are less likely than men to remain severely depressed or socially isolated after the death of a spouse.[15]

There are many possible explanations for these sex differences in response to widowhood. Women may remarry less because they have greater loyalty to the dead spouse. Women may be more timid in seeking out romantic-sexual partners than are men. Also, male marriage partners are in much greater demand than are female partners because of the scarcity of older males (due both to longevity differences between the sexes and to the pairing of older men with younger women). Another explanation lies in the nature of sex-role training throughout the life cycle. Men are generally not socialized to establish close personal ties with individuals outside the immediate family. In order to get their emotional needs met, they often must regain a marriage partner with whom it is socially acceptable to share feelings. In contrast, women are socialized to share emotions with a whole range of people, including nonrelated peers.

Women are less dependent on their spouses than men are for getting their emotional needs met. One woman, my grand-mother, who had been widowed for over five years was asked if she had considered remarrying. "Who, me?" she said, in an astonished voice. "I was married once and that's enough. I don't want to serve another man and his children." She lived as a widow for fourteen years and had an extraordinarily rich social life, filled with close friends and family and many activities. Most women have social skills that enable them to live alone in later adulthood somewhat more easily and more successfully than most men.

In old age, people suffer the pain of frequently losing dear partners and friends to death. The loss of a spouse, the death of a lesbian or gay male partner, the death of a close friend, can be deeply diminishing. The way one deals with these sad realities will reflect the personality and social style developed in the years before old age.

Although elderly people suffer the loss of close friends and partners, they may also experience the pleasure of new relationships with grandchildren and great-grandchildren. While being a grandparent may make one feel older, it also offers many opportunities to share a special relationship featuring great affection and minimal responsibility. Grandparenting styles tend to shift with age and vary from person to person, but most people find the experience to be a rewarding aspect of aging. In some families, grandmothers spend a lot of time caring for and playing with their grandchildren. And grandfathers, who may have missed out on close contact with their own children due to early pressures to live up to the masculine ideal, may now have the time and inclination to enjoy nurturing young family members.

Sexuality

Contrary to social mythology, it is healthy and normal for older people to express and explore their sexuality. Unfortunately, many older people accept stereotypes and consider their own extensive and normal sexual needs to be deviant and embarrassing. Old people may also feel particularly unattractive because they diverge so markedly from youthful standards of beauty. A deteriorating self-image can lead to anxiety over seeking sexual fulfillment. A group of researchers interviewed men and women in their eighties and nineties. These respondents reported having mild or moderate interest in sex. Often they found their interest was greater than their actual sexual activity because of a lack of partners.[16] Progressively with age, men and women need greater sexual stimulation but are quite capable of orgasm and of extensive sexual pleasure. This is a period of sexuality in which tenderness and sensitivity to mutual needs are most central to sexual enjoyment. Despite fears of loss of attractiveness, both men and women bloom sexually with an accepting and loving partner. The same person who may have experienced a rigid and joyless sex life earlier, can have a fun-loving and pleasurable sexual relationship later in life with a more attentive lover.

Today there are many more older adults who are healthier, better educated, and better informed than in previous generations. They are able to enjoy their health and have the vigor to express themselves sexually. They are also more aware of the normality and importance of their sexual needs and thus feel more comfortable getting those needs met, both in and outside of marriage and/or long-term relationships. Often freer sexuality comes with the question, "What have I got to lose? Why not enjoy myself?" Not that all seniors lead exotic sex lives. But many are interested in having relationships which will affirm them emotionally, socially, and sexually. With the close-range perspective of their own mortality, perhaps older adults now wish to have what they denied themselves before. Even among nursing home residents, the demand for the right to have sexual relations in private places has been articulated in recent years.[17]

Many older adults increasingly engage in masturbation as an important form of sexual pleasure and release. It is a normal and common form of sexual expression that increases as sexual partners become less available.[18] Yet because of our society's negative view toward masturbation in general (especially for women) and toward sex for older people, many older adults feel guilty and behave furtively about their sexual activities.

Sex Roles and Social Change

Studying sex-role development in old age shows what can happen to individuals when economic roles diminish and change. Without the economic underpinnings, the mechanism of sex roles begins to lose its function; thus the marked increase in sex-role blending in old age. Looking at the whole life cycle, we can see the central importance of sex roles in influencing our personal and social lives. From birth until death individuals are labeled by sex as well as by social class, race, ethnicity, and sexual preference. People in these different social categories have different opportunities, responsibilities, and privileges. The desire to "fit in" and be accepted makes most people very open and vulnerable to the culture's demands of obedience to roles in general and sex roles in particular. Consequently, males and females often eagerly participate in the processes of becoming masculine and becoming feminine throughout the life cycle. All the while, however, men and women are changing these sex roles to suit their own perceived needs and the needs of the changing economic and social system.

In recent years, the women's movement has publicly raised questions about women's and men's roles in society. Increasingly, researchers have considered the complexity of sex roles. Further research will help illuminate these complexities of social and personality development of individuals in our social structure. It is impossible, now, to return to totally traditional sex roles, because the social conditions spawning those roles no longer exist. We must go on modifying behavior and attitudes while recognizing the many influences of past sex-role socialization. And by analyzing how the social, economic, and cultural conditions continue to affect us as females and males, we can attempt to change those aspects of society that limit our potential as human beings.

About the Author

NANCY ROMER is an assistant professor of psychology at Brooklyn College of The City University of New York, where she also teaches in the women's studies program. Romer, who has a Ph.D. in psychology and education from the University of Michigan, has published articles on sex roles in a number of journals, including *Developmental Psychology*, *Psychology of Women Quarterly*, and *Sex Roles: A Journal of Research*. She has been active in the women's movement for many years.

A Note on Language

IN EDITING BOOKS, The Feminist Press attempts to eliminate harmful sex and race bias inherent in the language. In order to retain the authenticity of historical and literary documents, however, our policy is to leave their original language unaltered. We recognize that the task of changing language usage is extremely complex and that it will not be easily accomplished. The process is an ongoing one that we share with many others concerned with the relationship between a humane language and a more humane world.

Notes

Introduction

1. Philippe Ariès, *Centuries of Childhood* (New York: Alfred A. Knopf, 1962).

2. Bureau of the Census, *Statistical Abstract of the United States—1977: National Data Book and Guide to Sources* (Washington, D.C.: U.S. Department of Commerce, Bureau of the Census, 1977).

3. Melvin Kohn, "Social Class and Parental Values," *American Journal of Sociology* 44 (1959) : 337–51.

4. Anna Nieto-Gomez, "Heritage of La Hembra," in *Female Psychology: The Emerging Self*, ed. Sue Cox (Chicago: Science Research Associates, 1976), pp. 226–35; Evelyn P. Steven, "Marianismo: The Other Face of Machismo in Latin America," *The Western Political Quarterly*, December 1965.

5. Irene Fujitomi and Diane Wong, "The New Asian-American Woman," in *Female Psychology*, ed. Cox pp. 236–48.

6. Joseph P. Fitzpatrick, *Puerto Rican Americans: The Meaning of Migration to the Mainland* (Englewood Cliffs, N.J.: Prentice-Hall, 1971); Alfonso Pinkney, *Black Americans* (Englewood Cliffs, N.J.: Prentice-Hall, 1976); and Joseph Lopreato, *Italian Americans* (New York: Random House, 1970).

7. Cynthia Fuchs Epstein, *Woman's Place: Options and Limits in Professional Careers* (Berkeley, Calif.: University of California Press, 1971).

8. Pauline Bart, "Depression in Middle-Aged Women," in *Women in Sexist Society*, eds. Vivian Gornick and Barbara K. Moran (New York: Basic Books, 1971).

9. E.R. Carlson and R. Carlson, "Male and Female Subjects in Personality Research," *Journal of Abnormal and Social Psychology* 60 (1960): 482–83; and D.S. Holmes and B.W. Jorgensen, "Do Personality and Social Psychologists Study More Men than Women?" *Representative Research in Social Psychology* 2 (1971): 71–76.

10. A number of excellent critical reviews of psychological research in this area have been written. For example, see Mary Brown Parlee, "Psychology and Women," *Signs* 5, no. 1 (Autumn 1979): 121–33; Irene H. Frieze, Jacquelynne E. Parsons, Paula B. Johnson, Diane N. Ruble, and Gail L. Zellman, *Women and Sex Roles: A Social Psychological Perspective* (New York: W.W. Norton & Co., 1978), especially chapter 2, "Doing Psychological Research," pp. 11–27; and Nancy Romer and Elyse Sutherland, review of *Fear of Success* by David Tresemer, *Psychology of Women Quarterly*, 1980 in press.

One: Infancy

1. Listen, for example, to "Soliloquy," from Richard Rodgers and Oscar Hammerstein's musical *Oklahoma!*

2. Michael Lewis, "Parents and Children: Sex-Role Developments," *School Review* 80, no. 2 (February 1972): 229–40.

3. Jeffrey Z. Rubin, Frank Provenzano, and Zella Luria, "The Eye of the Beholder: Parents' Views on Sex of Newborns," *American Journal of Orthopsychiatry* 44, no. 4 (1974): 512–19.

4. Howard A. Moss, "Sex, Age and Status as Determinants of Mother-Infant Interaction," *Merrill-Palmer Quarterly* 13, no. 1 (1967): 19–36; R. Parke, S. O'Leary, and S. West,

"Mother-Father-Newborn Interaction: Effects of Maternal Medication, Labor, and Sex of Infant," *Proceedings of the 80th Annual Convention of the American Pyschological Association, 1972;* Lewis, "Parents and Children"; Michael Lewis and Marcia Weintraub, "Sex of Parent x Sex of Child: Socioemotional Development," in *Sex Differences in Behavior,* eds. R.D. Friedman, R.M. Richart, and R.C. Vandewiele (New York: John Wiley & Sons, 1974), pp. 165–90; Susan Goldberg and Michael Lewis, "Play Behavior in the Year-Old Infant: Early Sex Differences," *Child Development* 40 (1969): 21–32. Lewis and colleagues found that mothers touch, hold, rock, and kiss their sons more than their daughters between zero and six months of age, though this trend reverses itself in the next six months. They conclude that in the first years of life, boys are gradually weaned off physical contact while girls are not.

5. Jerome Kagan, *Change and Continuity in Infancy* (New York: John Wiley & Sons, 1971); Howard A. Moss, "Early Sex Differences and Mother-Infant Interaction," in *Sex Differences in Behavior,* eds. Friedman, Richart, and Vandewiele.

6. Robert R. Sears, Eleanor E. Maccoby, and Harry Levin, *Patterns of Child Rearing* (Evanston, Ill.: Row, Peterson & Co., 1957).

7. Juanita H. Williams, *Psychology of Women: Behavior in a Biosocial Context* (New York: W.W. Norton & Co., 1977); Shirley Weitz, *Sex Roles: Biological, Psychological and Social Foundations* (New York: Oxford University Press, 1977).

8. J.M. Tanner, "Physical Growth," in *Charmichael's Manual of Child Psychology,* ed. P.H. Mussen, 3d ed., vol. 1 (New York: John Wiley & Sons, 1970), pp. 77–156.

9. J.E. Garai and A. Scheinfeld,

"Sex Differences in Mental and Behavioral Traits," *Genetic Psychology Monographs* 77 (1968): 169–299. Two possible explanations are offered for the apparently greater hardiness of the female newborn. Some biologists believe that the X chromosome not only has more genetic material than the Y chromosome but may also have many abnormalities; because the male does not have a second X chromosome that may offer dominant and healthy traits to offset the negative effects of the first X chromosome, the male is more likely to have defective characteristics. Other biologists believe that the male, due to his Y chromosome, may develop characteristics that are incompatible with the mother in whom he is developing. This incompatability may lead to problems in development and in the birth process.

10. Anneliese F. Korner, "Methodological Considerations in Studying Sex Differences in the Behavioral Functioning of Newborns," in *Sex Differences in Behavior,* eds. Friedman, Richart, and Vandewiele.

11. Anne Oakley, *Sex, Gender and Society* (South Melbourne, Australia: Sun Books, 1972).

12. Eleanor E. Maccoby and Carol N. Jacklin, *The Psychology of Sex Differences* (Stanford, Calif.: Stanford University Press, 1974).

13. Kagan, *Change and Continuity in Infancy.*

14. Jerome Kagan and Howard Moss, *Birth to Maturity* (New York: John Wiley & Sons, 1962).

15. Goldberg and Lewis, "Play Behavior in the Year-Old Infant."

16. Maccoby and Jacklin, *The Psychology of Sex Differences;* Tanner, "Physical Growth."

17. Sears, Maccoby, and Levin, *Patterns of Child Rearing.*

18. Jean D. Grambs and Walter B. Waetjen, *Sex: Does It Make a Difference?* (Belmont, Calif.: Duxbury Press, 1975).

19. Harriet Rheingold and K. V. Cook, "The Contents of Boys' and Girls' Rooms as an Index of Parents' Behavior," *Child Development* 46, no. 2 (1975): 459–63.

20. Mary K. Rothbart and Eleanor E. Maccoby, "Parents' Differential Reactions to Sons and Daughters,"*Journal of Personality and Social Psychology* 4, no. 3 (1966): 237–45.

21. Ibid.

22. Kagan, *Change and Continuity in Infancy.*

23. John Money, "Ablatio Penis: Normal Male Infant Sex-Reassignment as a Girl," *Archives of Sexual Behavior* 4, no. 1 (1975): 65–71.

24. Nancy Chodorow, *The Reproduction of Mothering: Psychoanalysis and the Sociology of Gender* (Berkeley, Calif.: University of California Press, 1978); Dorothy Dinnerstein, *The Mermaid and the Minotaur* (New York: Colophon Books, 1977).

Two: Early Childhood

1. Eleanor E. Maccoby and Carol N. Jacklin, *The Psychology of Sex Differences* (Stanford, Calif.: Stanford University Press, 1974); Kenneth Clark, *Dark Ghetto* (New York: Harper & Row, 1965).

2. Jean Piaget, *The Origins of Intelligence* (New York: International Universities Press, 1952); Lawrence Kohlberg, "A Cognitive-Developmental Analysis of Children's Sex-Role Concepts and Attitudes," in *The Development of Sex Differences,* ed. Eleanor E. Maccoby (Stanford, Calif.: Stanford University Press, 1966).

3. Kohlberg, "A Cognitive-Developmental Analysis"; Lenore A. Delucia, "The Toy-Preference Test: A Measure of Sex-Role Identification," *Child Development* 34 (1963): 107–17.

4. Nancy Romer and Debra Cherry, "Multiple Influences on Children's Sex Role Concepts," unpublished manuscript, Brooklyn College, 1977.

5. Harriet Rheingold and Kaye V. Cook, "The Contents of Boys' and Girls' Rooms as an Index of Parents' Behavior," *Child Development* 46, no. 2 (1975): 459–63.

6. Anne Berens, "The Socialization of Need for Achievement in Boys and Girls," *American Psychological Association Proceedings,* vol. 7, pt. 1 (1972), pp. 273–74; Susan Saegart and Roger Hart, "The Development of Sex Differences in the Environmental Competence of Children," in *Women in Society,* ed. P. Burnett (Chicago: Maaroufa Press, 1976); Beverly Fagot, "Sex Differences in Toddler's Behavior and Parental Reaction," *Developmental Psychology* 10 (1974): 554–58.

7. Jean D. Grambs and Walter B. Waetjen, *Sex: Does It Make a Difference?* (Belmont, Calif.: Duxbury Press, 1975).

8. Jerome Kagan and Howard Moss, *Birth to Maturity* (New York: John Wiley & Sons, 1962).

9. Lois Wladis Hoffman, "Early Childhood Experiences and Women's Achievement Motives," *Journal of Social Issues* 28, no. 2 (1972) : 129–55.

10. Bureau of the Census, *Statistical Abstract of the United States-1977: National Data Book and Guide to Sources* (Washington, D.C.: U.S. Department of Commerce, Bureau of the Census); Betty Friedan, "Feminism Takes a New Turn," *The New York Times Magazine,* 18 November 1979.

11. Nancy Romer and Debra Cherry, "Task Sharing and Maternal Employment in the 1970s," unpublished manuscript, Brooklyn College, 1977.

12. Kohlberg, "A Cognitive-Developmental Analysis"; Ulf Hannerz, *Soulside: Inquiries into Ghetto Culture and Community* (New York: Columbia University Press, 1969).

13. E. Mavis Hetherington and J. Deur, "The Effects of Father Absence on Child Development," in *The Young Child: Reviews of Research*, ed. W.W. Hartup, vol. 2 (Washington, D.C.: National Association for the Education of Young Children, 1972), pp. 303–19; David B. Lynn and W.L. Sawrey, "The Effects of Father Absence on Norwegian Boys and Girls," *Journal of Abnormal and Social Psychology* 59 (1959) : 258–62.

14. Walter Mischel, "Sex-Typing and Socialization," in *Carmichael's Manual of Child Psychology*, ed. P.H Mussen, 3d ed., vol. 2 (New York: John Wiley & Sons, 1970); Lynn and Sawrey, "The Effects of Father Absence."

15. E. Mavis Hetherington, "Effects of Father Absence on Personality Development in Adolescent Daughters," *Developmental Psychology* 7 (1972): 313–26.

16. E. Hilberman and K. Munson, "Sixty Battered Women: A Preliminary Report," paper delivered at the American Psychiatric Association Meeting, May 1977.

17. Benjamin George Rosenberg and Brian Sutton-Smith, "Family Interaction Effects on Masculinity-Femininity," *Journal of Personality and Social Psychology* 8 (1968): 117–20.

18. Jerry Mander, *Four Arguments for the Elimination of Television* (New York: William Morrow & Co., 1978).

19. Sarah H. Sternglanz and Lisa A. Serbin, "Sex-Role Stereotyping in Children's Television Programs," *Developmental Psychology* 10, no.5 (1974) : 710–15.

20. Jane Bergman, "Are Little Girls Being Harmed by 'Sesame Street'? in *And Jill Came Tumbling After: Sexism in American Education*, eds. Judith Stacey, Susan Bereaud, and Joan Daniels (New York: Dell Publishing Co., 1974).

21. "A Report on Children's Toys," in Stacey, Bereaud, and Daniels, eds., *And Jill Came Tumbling After*.

22. Lucy Komisar, "The Image of Women in Advertising," in *Women in Sexist Society*, eds. Vivian Gornick and Barbara K. Moran (New York: Basic Books, 1971).

23. Beverly Fagot and Gerald R. Patterson, "An *In Vivo* Analysis of Reinforcing Contingencies for Sex-Role Behaviors in the Preschool Child," *Developmental Psychology* no. 5 (1969): 563–68.

24. Carole Joffe, "Sex Role Socialization and the Nursery School: As the Twig Is Bent," *Journal of Marriage and the Family* 33, no. 3 (1971) : 467–75.

25. Lisa Serbin, "Teachers, Peers and Play Preferences: An Environmental Approach to Sex-Typing in the Preschool," in *Perspectives on Non-Sexist Early Childhood Education*, ed. Barbara Sprung (New York: Teachers College Press, 1978), p.80.

26. Ibid.; L.A. Serbin, D.K. O'Leary, R.N. Kent, and I.J. Tonick, "A Comparison of Teacher Responses to the Pre-Academic and Problem Behavior of Boys and Girls," *Child Development* 44 (1972) : 796–804.

27. Joffe, "Sex Role Socialization"; Barbara Grizzuti Harrison,

Unlearning the Lie: Sexism in School (New York: William Morrow & Co, 1974).

28. Lenore Weitzman, Deborah Eifler, Elizabeth Hokada, and Catherine Ross, "Sex Role Socialization in Picture Books for Preschool Children," *American Journal of Sociology* 77, no. 6 (1972) : 1125-50.

29. Phyllis Taube Greenleaf, *Liberating Young Children From Sex Roles: Experience in Day Care Centers, Play Groups and Free Schools* (Somerville, Mass.: New England Free Press, 1972).

30. Kohlberg, "A Cognitive-Developmental Analysis."

31. Walter Mischel, "A Social Learning View of Sex Differences in Behavior," in *The Development of Sex Differences,* ed. Maccoby.

32. Sigmund Freud, "Some Physical Consequences of the Anatomical Distinction Between the Sexes" (1925), in *Standard Edition of the Complete Psychological Works of Sigmund Freud,* ed. and trans. James Strachey (London: Hogarth Press); Erik Erikson, *Childhood and Society* (New York: W. W. Norton & Co., 1963).

Three: Childhood

1. Jean Piaget, *The Origins of Intelligence* (New York: International Universities Press, 1952).

2. Erik Erikson, *Childhood and Society* (New York: W. W. Norton & Co., 1963).

3. Roger Hart, "Sex Differences in the Use of Outdoor Space," in *Perspectives on Non-Sexist Early Childhood Education,* ed. Barbara Sprung (New York: Teachers College Press, 1978).

4. Marc Feigen Fasteau, *The Male Machine* (New York: Dell Publishing Co., 1957), p. 104.

5. Eleanor E. Maccoby and Carol N. Jacklin, *The Psychology of Sex Differences* (Stanford, Calif.: Stanford University Press, 1974).

6. Melvin John, "Social Class and Parental Values," *American Journal of Sociology* 44 (1959) : 337–51; Urie Bronfenbrenner, "Socialization and Social Class Through Time and Space," in *The Impact of Social Class,* ed. Paul Blumberg (New York: Thomas Y. Crowell Company, 1972), pp. 381–409; Lillian B. Rubin, *Worlds of Pain: Life in the Working Class Family* (New York: Basic Books, 1976).

7. Meyer L. Rabban, "Sex Role Identifiction in Young Children in Two Diverse Social Groups," *Genetic Psychology Monographs* 42 (1950): 81–158; Nancy Romer and Debra Cherry, "Ethnic and Social Class Differences in Children's Sex Role Concepts," *Sex Roles: A Journal of Research,* no. 2 (Spring 1980): 245—63.

8. Nancy Romer, "The Motive to Avoid Success and its Effects on Performance in School-Aged Males and Females," *Developmental Psychology* 2, no. 6 (1975) : 689-99.

9. Lawrence Kohlberg, "A Cognitive-Developmental Analysis of Children's Sex-Role Concepts and Attitudes," in *The Development of Sex Differences,* ed. Eleanor E. Maccoby (Stanford, Calif.: Stanford University Press, 1960).

10. Judith M. Bardwick and Elizabeth Douvan, "Ambivalence: The Socialization of Women," in *Women in Sexist Society,* eds. Vivian Gornick and Barbara Moran (New York: Basic Books, 1971).

11. Karen Horney, *Feminine Psychology* (New York: W. W. Norton & Co., 1967).

12. Jerome Kagan, "The Child's Sex Role Classification of School Objects," *Child Development* 35 (1964) : 1051-56.

13. Eleanor Leacock, *Teaching and Learning in City Schools* (New York: Basic Books, 1969).

14. Karen Branan, "What Can I do About...Sex Discrimination?" *Scholastic Teacher: Elementary School Teacher's Edition* (November 1971), p. 20.

15. Frances Bentzen, "Sex Ratios in Learning and Behavior Disorders," *The National Elementary Principal* 46, no. 2 (1966) : 13–17; Eleanor E. Maccoby, "Sex Differences in Intellectual Functioning," in *The Development of Sex Differences*, ed. Maccoby.

16. Lois Wladis Hoffman, "Early Childhood Experiences and Women's Achievement Motives," *Journal of Social Issues* 28, no.2 (1972) : 129–55.

17. Helen Felsenthal, "Pupils' Sex as a Variable in Teacher Perceptions of Classroom Behavior," paper delivered at the American Educational Research Association Convention, 1971.

18. Helen Felsenthal, "Sex Differences in Teacher-Pupil Interaction During First Grade Reading Instruction," paper delivered at the American Educational Research Association Convention, 1970; Robert L. Spaulding, "Achievement, Creativity, and Self-Concept Correlates of Teacher-Pupil Transactions in Elementary Schools," Cooperative Research Project No. 1352 (Washington, D.C.: U.S. Department of Health, Education and Welfare, Office of Education, 1963).

19. Spaulding, "Achievement, Creativity, and Self-Concept"; Carol S. Dweck and E.S. Bush, "Sex Differences in Learned Helplessness: Differential Debilitation with Peer and Adult Evaluators," *Developmental Psychology* 12 (1976): 147–56.

20. Nancy Frazier and Myra Sadker, *Sexism in School and Society* (New York: Harper & Row, 1973).

21. Marjorie B. U'ren, "The Image of Women in Textbooks," in *Women in Sexist Society*, eds. Gornick and Moran.

22. Women on Words and Images, *Dick and Jane as Victims* (Princeton, N.J.: Women on Words and Images, 1972).

23. Marcia Federbush, *Let Them Aspire: A Plea and Proposal for Equality of Opportunity for Males and Females in the Ann Arbor Public Schools* (Pittsburgh, Pa.: KNOW Inc., 1971).

24. Marcia Guttentag and Helen Bray, *Undoing Sex Stereotypes: Research and Resources for Educators* (New York: McGraw-Hill Book Company, 1976).

25. Barbara Grizutti Harrison, *Unlearning the Lie* (New York: William Morrow & Co., 1974).

26. Lois W. Hoffman, "Early Childhood Experiences"; H.J. Walberg, "Physics, Femininity and Creativity," *Developmental Psychology* 1 (1969) : 47–54.

27. Virginia J. Crandall and A. Rabson, "Children's Repetition Choices in an Intellectual Achievement Situation Following Success and Failure," *Journal of Genetic Psychology* 97 (1960) : 161–68.

Four: Adolescence

1. Margene S. Faust, "Developmental Maturity as a Determinant in Prestige of Adolescent Girls," *Child Development* 31 (1960) : 173–84; Mary Cover Jones, "Psychological Correlates of Somatic Development," *Child Development* 36 (1965) : 899–911.

2. William H. Grier and Price M. Cobb, *Black Rage* (New York: Basic Books, 1968).

3. Joyce Ladner, *Tomorrow's Tomorrow* (Garden City, N.Y.: Doubleday & Co., 1972); Gloria J. Powell, "Self-Concept in White and Black Children," in *Racism and Mental Health*, eds. Charles V. Willie, Bernard M. Kramer, and Bertram S. Brown (Pittsburgh: University of Pittsburgh Press, 1973); Carol B. Stack, "Sex Roles and Survival Strategies in an Urban Black Community," in *Women, Culture and Society*, eds. Michelle Z. Rosaldo and Louise Lamphere (Stanford, Calif.: Stanford University Press, 1974).

4. Eugene Bliss, "Anorexia Nervosa," *Comprehensive Textbook of Psychiatry*, 2d ed., vol. 2 (Baltimore: The Williams & Wilkins Company, 1975); Hilde Bruch, *The Golden Cage: The Enigma of Anorexia Nervosa* (Cambridge, Mass.: Harvard University Press, 1978).

5. Gisela Konopka, *Young Girls: A Portrait of Adolescence* (Englewood Cliffs, N.J.: Prentice-Hall, 1976).

6. Trial of Inez Garcia, August 1974, transcript enacted on WNET-TV, 25 May 1977. Another judge, in Madison, Wisconsin, stated as a response to a charge of rape committed by a fifteen-year-old male, "The youth's action was a normal response to women's provocative clothing and behavior." *The New York Times*, 9 September 1977. This judge was later recalled for his prejudiced point of view.

7. Lynda Holstrom and Anne Burgess, *The Victim of Rape: Institutional Reactions* (New York: Interscience, 1978).

8. Grace Lichtenstein, "Rape Laws Undergoing Changes to Aide Victims," *The New York Times*, 4 June 1975.

9. Konopka, *Young Girls*.

10. Lillian B. Rubin, *Worlds of Pain: Life in the Working Class Family* (New York: Basic Books, 1976); Lillian B. Rubin, *Women of a Certain Age: The Midlife Search for Self* (New York: Harper & Row, 1979).

11. Anne McCreary Juhasz, "Changing Patterns of Premarital Sexual Behavior," in *Focus: Human Sexuality 77/78*, ann. ed. (Guilford, Conn.: The Dushkin Publishing Group, 1977).

12. William Simon and John H. Gagnon, "On Psychosexual Development," in *Handbook of Socialization Theory and Research*, ed. David A. Goslin (Chicago: Rand McNally & Company, 1969).

13. Shere Hite, *The Hite Report: A Nationwide Survey of Female Sexuality* (New York: Dell Publishing Co., 1976).

14. Clellan S. Ford and Frank A. Beach, *Patterns of Sexual Behavior* (New York: Colophon Books, 1951); M. Freedman, *Homosexuality and Psychological Functioning* (Monterey, Calif.: Brooks/Cole Publishing Company, 1971); K. Mannion, "Female Homosexuality: A Comprehensive Review of Theory and Research," *JSAS Catalogue of Selected Documents in Psychology* 6, no. 1 (1978) : 44.

15. Herant Katchadourian and Donald Lunde, *Fundamentals of Human Sexuality*, 2 ed. (New York: Holt, Rinehart & Winston, 1975).

16. D. H. Rosen, *Lesbianism: A Study of Female Homosexuality* (Springfield, Ill.: Charles C. Thomas, Publisher, 1974).

17. Alan P. Bell and Martin S. Weinberg, *Homosexualities: A Study of Diversity Among Men and Women* (New York: Simon &

Schuster, 1978); Barry Dank, "Coming Out in the Gay World," *Psychiatry* 34 (1971) : 180–97.

18. Sasha Gregory Lewis, *Sunday's Women: A Report on Lesbian Life Today* (Boston: Beacon Press, 1979); Ginny Vida, ed., *Our Right to Love: A Lesbian Resource Book* (Englewood Cliffs, N.J.: Prentice-Hall, 1978); Jonathan Katz, *Gay American History: Lesbians and Gay Men in the U.S.A.* (New York: Thomas Y. Crowell Company, 1976).

19. Bell and Weinberg, *Homosexualities.*

20. Ibid.; Lewis, *Sunday's Women;* Vida, *Our Right to Love.*

21. Lewis, *Sunday's Women;* Charlotte Wolff, *Love Between Women* (New York: St. Martin's Press, 1971).

22. Wolff, *Love Between Women;* Marilyn G. Fleener, "The Lesbian Lifestyle," paper presented at the Western Social Science Association, April 1977.

23. Vida, *Our Right to Love.*

24. Dank, "Coming Out."

25. Margaret Mead, *Coming of Age in Samoa: A Psychological Study of Primitive Youth for Western Civilization* (New York: Dell Publishing Co., 1968).

26. Konopka, *Young Girls.*

27. Joseph P. Fitzpatrick, *Puerto Rican Americans: The Meaning of Migration to the Mainland* (Englewood Cliffs, N.J.: Prentice-Hall, 1971).

28. Rubin, *Worlds of Pain.*

29. Ibid.

30. James S. Coleman, *The Adolescent Society: The Social Life of the Teenager and Its Impact on Education* (New York: Free Press, 1961); Alfonso Pinkney, *Black Americans* (Englewood Cliffs, N.J.: Prentice-Hall, 1975).

31. Nancy Romer and Debra Cherry, "Ethnic and Social Class Differences in Children's Sex Role Concepts," *Sex Roles: A Journal of Research* 6, no. 2 (Spring 1980): 245–63; Andrew Billingsley, *Black Families in White America* (Englewood Cliffs, N.J.: Prentice-Hall, 1971); Joseph A. Ryan, ed., *White Ethnics: Life in Working-Class America* (Englewood Cliffs, N.J.: Prentice-Hall, 1973).

32. Judith M. Bardwick and Elizabeth Douvan, "Ambivalence: The Socialization of Women," in *Women in Sexist Society,* eds. Vivian Gornick and Barbara Moran (New York: Basic Books, 1971).

33. Matina S. Horner, "Femininity and Successful Achievement: A Basic Inconsistency," in *Feminine Personality and Conflicts,* eds. J. Bardwick et al. (Belmont, Calif.: Brooks/Cole Publishing Company, 1970).

34. Nancy Romer, "The Motive to Avoid Success and Its Effects on Performance in School-Aged Males and Females," *Developmental Psychology* 11, no. 6 (1975): 689–99.

35. Lois Wladis Hoffman, "Fear of Success in Males and Females: 1965 and 1971," *Journal of Consulting and Clinical Psychology* 42 (1974): 129–56.

36. Mirra Komarovsky, *Dilemmas of Masculinity: A Study of College Youth* (New York: W. W. Norton & Co., 1976).

37. Bardwick and Douvan, "Ambivalence."

38. Betty Friedan, *The Feminine Mystique* (New York: Dell Publishing Co., 1963).

39. Lois Wladis Hoffman, "Changes in Family Roles, Socialization and Sex Differences," *American Psychologist* 2, no. 8 (1977): 644–57.

40. Peter J. Weston and Martha T. Mednick,"Race, Social Class, and the Motive to Avoid Success in

Women," *Journal of Cross-Cultural Psychology* 1, no. 3 (1970): 284–91.

41. Ladner, *Tomorrow's Tomorrow*.

42. C. B. Thoy, "Status, Race, and Aspirations: A Study of the Desire of High School Students to Enter a Profession or a Technical Occupation," *Dissertation Abstracts International* 2 (10-A, 1969), abs. no. 3672.

43. Alice de Rivera, "On Desegregating Stuyvesant High," in *Sisterhood Is Powerful*, ed. Robin Morgan (New York: Vintage Books, 1970).

44. G. A. Milton, *Five Studies of the Relation Between Sex Role Identification and Achievement in Problem Solving*, Technical Report no. 3, Department of Industrial Administration, Department of Psychology, Yale University, December 1958.

45. Elizabeth Fennema and Julia Sherman, "Sex-Related Differences in Mathematics Achievement: Spatial Visualization and Affective Actors," *American Educational Research Journal* 14, no.1 (Winter 1977):66

46. Robert Kerchoff, *Socialization and Social Class* (Englewood Cliffs, N.J.: Prentice-Hall, 1976); Melvin Kohn, "Social Class and Parent-Child Relationships: An Interpretation," *American Journal of Sociology* 68 (1963): 471–80.

47. Joseph R. Bard, ed., *Sexism in Education: Joint Task Force* (Harrisburg: Pennsylvania Department of Education, 1972); Janice Law Trecker, "Women in U.S. History High School Textbooks," *Social Education* 35 (1971): 249–61; Sandy Weinbaum, "Women in High School U.S. History Texts: Where Are the Changes," *Women's Studies Newsletter* 7, no. 2 (Spring 1979): 4—7; Katz, *Gay American History*.

48. Catherine D. Lyon and Terry N. Saario, "Women in Public Education: Sex Discrimination in Promotions," *Phi Delta Kappa* 54 (1973): 123–40.

49. Women's Action Alliance, *Women's Action Almanac*, eds. Jane Williamson, Diane Winston, and Wanda Wooton (New York: William Morrow and Company, 1980), p.107.

50. Nancy Frazier and Myra Sadker, *Sexism in School and Society* (New York: Harper & Row, 1973), p. 147.

51. Florence Howe, *Seven Years Later: Women's Studies Programs in 1976* (Washington, D.C.: National Advisory Council on Women's Educational Programs, 1977); "Women's Studies Programs—1980," *Women's Studies Newsletter* 8, no. 1 (Winter 1980): 19–26.

52. Miriam Gilbert, "Women in Medicine," in *Sisterhood is Powerful*, ed. Robin Morgan (New York: Vintage Books, 1970).

53. Women's Action Alliance, *Women's Action Almanac*, p. 107.

54. National Commission on the Observance of Women's Year, *What Women Want* (New York: Simon and Schuster, 1979), p. 160.

55. "Women: The Fight for a Fair Shake on Campus," *The New York Times*, 8 October 1972; Jack Margarell, "Who Earns How Much in Academe," *Chronicle of Higher Education* 9, no. 19 (1974).

56. Frazier and Sadker, *Sexism in School and Society*.

57. Komarovsky,*Dilemmas of Masculinity*.

58. Alice Rossi, "Barriers to the Career Choice of Engineering, Medicine or Science Among American Women," in *Readings on the Psychology of Women*, ed. Judith M. Bardwick (New York: Harper & Row, 1972).

59. David Tresemer, *Fear of Success* (New York: Plenum

Publishing Corporation, 1978); Susan Romer Kaplan, "Why Would a Woman over Thirty-Five Want to Go to Medical School?" unpublished manuscript, University of California, Berkeley, 1980; Robert J. Braun, *Teachers and Power* (New York: Simon and Schuster, 1972).

Five: Young Adulthood

1. M.N. Reedy, "Love, Sexuality and Aging," in *Sexuality and Aging*, eds., I.N. Burnside and R. Solnick (Los Angeles: University of Southern California Press, 1978); Judith Long Laws and Pepper Schwartz, *Sexual Scripts* (Kinsdale, Ill.: Dryden Press, 1977); Carol Tavris, "Men and Women Report Their Views on Masculinity," *Psychology Today* 10 (January 1977): 34–42, 82.

2. Phillip Shaver and Jonathan Freedman, "Your Pursuit of Happiness," *Psychology Today* 10 (August 1976): 26–32, 75; *Work in America*, Report of a Special Task Force to the Secretary of Health, Education and Welfare (Cambridge, Mass.: M.I.T. Press, 1973); Francine E. Gordon and D.T. Hall, "Self-Image and Stereotypes of Femininity: Their Relationship to Women's Role Conflicts and Coping," *Journal of Applied Psychiatry* 59 (1974): 241–43.

3. Joseph Lopreato, *Italian Americans* (New York: Random House, 1970); Alphonso Pinkney, *Black Americans* (Englewood Cliffs, N.J.: Prentice-Hall, 1975).

4. Bernice K. Neugarten, ed., *Middle Age and Aging* (Chicago: University of Chicago Press, 1968); Lillian B. Rubin, *Worlds of Pain: Life in the Working-Class Family* (New York: Basic Books, 1976).

5. Mirra Komarovsky, *Dilemmas of Masculinity: A Study of College Youth* (New York: W.W. Norton & Co., 1976).

6. Myra Marx Ferree, "Working Class Jobs: Housework and Paid Work as Sources of Satisfaction," *Social Problems* 23 (1976): 431–41. Rubin, *Worlds of Pain*.

7. Eli Zaretsky, *Capitalism, the Family and Personal Life* (New York: Colophon Books, 1976).

8. Karl E. Taeuber and James A. Sweet, "Family and Work: The Social Life Cycle of Women," in *Women and the American Economy*, ed. Juanita M. Kreps (Englewood Cliffs, N.J.: Prentice-Hall, 1976); Bureau of the Census, *Statistical Abstract of the United States—1977: National Data Book and Guide to Sources* (Washington, D.C.: U.S. Department of Commerce, Bureau of the Census, 1977).

9. Laws and Schwartz, *Sexual Scripts*.

10. Jessie Bernard, "The Paradox of the Happy Marriage," in *Women in Sexist Society*, eds. Vivian Gornick and Barbara Moran (New York: Basic Books, 1971); Rubin, *Worlds of Pain*.

11. Genevieve Knupfer, Walter Clark, and Robin Room, "The Mental Health of the Unmarried," *American Journal of Psychiatry* 122 (1966): 841–51.

12. Zaretsky, *Capitalism, the Family and Personal Life*.

13. Rubin, *Worlds of Pain*, p. 105.

14. Sheila Rowbotham, *Woman's Consciousness, Man's World* (Baltimore: Penguin Books, 1973).

15. Mary Cahn Schwartz, "The High Price of 'Failure,'" *Lillith* 1, no. 1 (Fall 1976): 21–43; Erick Gronseth, "The Breadwinner Trap," in *The Future of the Family*, ed. Louise Knapp Howe (New York: Simon & Schuster, 1972).

16. Robert Gould, "Measuring Masculinity by the Size of a Paycheck," in *The Forty-Nine*

Percent Majority, eds. Deborah Davids and Robert Brannon (Reading, Mass.: Addison-Wesley Publishing Co., 1976); Gronseth, "The Breadwinner Trap."

17. John H. Scanzoni, *The Black Family in Modern Society: Patterns of Stability and Security* (Chicago: University of Chicago Press, 1977); Albert K. Cohen and Harold M. Hodges, Jr., "Characteristics of the Lower-Blue-Collar Class," *Social Problems* 10, no. 4 (1963): 303–10, 315–34; S. M. Miller and Frank Riessman, "The Working Class Subculture: A New View," *Social Problems* 9, no. 1 (Summer 1961): 86–97.

18. Phillip J. Stone, "Child Care in Twelve Countries," in *The Use of Time*, ed. Alexander Szalai (The Hague, The Netherlands: Mouton, 1972), pp. 249–64.

19. Suzanne K. Steinmetz and Murray K. Strauss, eds., *Violence in the Family* (New York: Dodd, Mead & Co., 1974); Maria Roy, ed., *Battered Women: A Psychosociological Study of Domestic Violence* (New York: Van Nostrand Reinhold Company, 1977); Del Martin, *Battered Wives* (New York: Pocket Books, 1977).

20. Knupfer, Clark, and Room, "The Mental Health of the Unmarried."

21. Alan P. Bell and Martin S. Weinberg, *Homosexualities: A Study of Diversity Among Men and Women* (New York: Simon and Schuster, 1978).

22. Phillip Blumstein and Pepper Schwartz, "Lesbianism and Bisexuality," in *Sexual Deviance and Sexual Deviants*, eds. E. Goods and R. Troiden (New York: William Morrow & Co., 1974); Mark Freedman, "Homosexuals May Be Healthier than Straights," *Psychology Today* (March 1975): 28–32.

23. Bell and Weinberg, *Homosexualities*.

24. Ginny Vida, ed., *Our Right to Love: A Lesbian Resource Book* (Englewood Cliffs, N.J.: Prentice-Hall, 1978); Blumstein and Schwartz, "Lesbianism and Bisexuality."

25. Lois Wladis Hoffman and Martin L. Hoffman, "The Value of Children to Parents," in *Psychological Perspectives on Fertility*, ed. J. T. Fawcett (New York: Basic Books, 1973); Marilyn Fabe and Norma Wikler, *Up Against the Clock: Career Women Speak on the Choice to Have Children* (New York: Random House, 1979).

26. Francis X. Clines, "Children of Desire," *The New York Times Magazine*, 30 September 1979.

27. Erik K. Erikson, *Identity: Youth and Crisis* (New York: W. W. Norton & Co., 1968).

28. Lillian E. Troll, *Early and Middle Adulthood* (Belmont, Calif.: Wadsworth Publishing Company, 1975).

29. Boston Women's Health Book Collective, *Ourselves and Our Children* (New York: Random House, 1978), p. 19.

30. Ibid., p. 27.

31. Ibid., p.19.

32. Ibid., p.24.

33. Ibid., p. 24.

34. One such organization is the National Organization for Non-Parents, 515 Madison Avenue, New York, N.Y. 10022.

35. Rochelle Semmel Albin,"The Healthy Adjustment of the Childless Woman," *Psychology Today* 13, no. 6 (November 1979): 29–30.

36. Joseph Veroff and Sheila Feld, *Marriage and Work in America: A Study of Motives and Roles* (New York: Van Nostrand Reinhold Company, 1970); Rubin, *Worlds of Pain*; also Lillian B. Rubin, *Women of a Certain Age: The Midlife Search*

for Self (New York: Harper & Row, 1979).

37. T. J. Keisner, "Fertility, Marital Instability and Alimony," paper presented at Eastern Economic Association, San Francisco, June 1975.

38. Lois Wladis Hoffman, "The Effects of the First Child on the Woman's Role," in The First Child and Family Formations, eds. W. Miller and L. Newman (Chapel Hill, N.C.: University of North Carolina Press, 1978).

39. Herbert J. Gans, The Urban Villagers: Group and Class in the Life of Italian-Americans (New York: Free Press of Glencoe, 1962); Joseph Lopreato, Italian Americans.

40. Carol B. Stack, All Our Kin: Strategies for Survival in a Black Community (New York: Colophon Books, 1974).

41. Rubin, Worlds of Pain.

42. Betty Friedan, The Feminine Mystique (New York: Dell Publishing Co., 1963); Shaver and Freedman, "Your Pursuit of Happiness."

43. Marian R. Yarrow et al., "Child-rearing in Families of Working and Nonworking Mothers," Sociometry 25 (June 1962): 122–40.

44. Myra Marx Ferree, "Working Class Jobs."

45. Judith A. Birnbaum, "Life Patterns, Personality Style and Self-Esteem in Gifted Family Oriented and Career Committed Women," unpublished doctoral dissertation, University of Michigan, 1971.

46. Robert O. Blood and David M. Wolfe, Husbands and Wives (New York: Free Press, 1960); Dair Gillespie, "Who Has the Power? The Marital Struggle," in Female Psychology: The Emerging Self, ed. Sue Cox (Chicago: Science Research Associates, 1976); pp. 192–211.

47. Lynda L. Holstrom, The Two Career Family (Cambridge, Mass.: Schenkman Publishing Co., 1972); Nancy Romer and Debra Cherry, "Task Sharing and Maternal Employment in the 1970's," unpublished manuscript, Brooklyn College, 1977.

48. Marion Gross Sobol, "Commitment to Work," in Working Mothers, eds. Lois Wladis Hoffman and F. Ivan Nye (San Francisco: Jossey-Bass Publishers, 1974), pp. 63–80; Ferree, "Working Class Jobs."

49. Rubin, Worlds of Pain.

50. Sandra S. Tangri, "Determinants of Occupational Role Innovation Among College Women," Journal of Social Issues 28, no. 2 (1972): 177–99; Ruth E. Hartley, "Children's Concepts of Male and Female Roles," Merrill Palmer Quarterly 6 (1960): 83–91; Ruth E. Hartley, "What Aspects of Child Behavior Should Be Studied in Relation to Maternal Employment?" in Research Issues Related to the Effects of Maternal Employment on Children, ed. A. E. Siegel (University Park, Pa.: Social Science Research Center, 1961).

51. Lois Wladis Hoffman,"Effects on Child," in Working Mothers, eds. Hoffman and Nye, pp. 126–66.

52. Rubin, Worlds of Pain.

53. David B. Lynn, The Father: His Role in Child Development (Monterey, Calif.: Brooks/Cole Publishing Company, 1974).

54. Barbara Rothberg, preliminary results of an interview study on joint-custody families, personal communication.

55. Fabe and Wikler, Up Against the Clock.

56. Vida, Our Right to Love; Sasha Gregory Lewis, Sunday's Women: A Report on Lesbian Life Today (Boston: Beacon Press, 1979).

57. Richard Green, Sexual Identity Conflict in Children and Adults (New York: Basic Books, 1974).

58. Vida, *Our Right to Love*; Brian Miller, "Uncompromised Paternity: The Life-Styles of Gay Fathers," in *Gay Men: The Sociology of Male Homosexuality*, ed. Martin P. Levine (New York: Colophon Books, 1979), pp. 239–42; Lewis, *Sunday's Women*.

59. Bell and Weinberg, *Homosexualities*.

60. Miller, "Uncompromised Paternity," pp. 239–52.

61. Vida, *Our Right to Love*; Lewis, *Sunday's Women*. Two organizations helping to fight such custody battles are Dykes and Tykes and The Lesbian Mothers Defense League.

62. K. Kincade, *A Walden Two Experiment: The First Five Years of Twin Oaks Community* (New York: William Morrow & Co., 1973); "Maryland Commune Defies Stereotype," *The New York Times*, 31 October 1976.

63. Zaretsky, *Capitalism, the Family and Personal Life*.

64. Nancy Chodorow, *The Reproduction of Mothering: Psychoanalysis and the Sociology of Gender* (Berkeley, Calif.: University of California Press, 1978).

65. Joyce Ladner, *Tomorrow's Tomorrow* (Garden City, N.Y.: Doubleday & Co., 1972).

66. Elizabeth Koltun, *The Jewish Woman* (New York: Schocken Books, 1978).

67. Bernice L. Neugarten, "Adult Personality: Toward a Psychology of the Life Cycle," in *Middle Age and Aging* (Chicago: University of Chicago Press, 1968).

68. Gabriel Kolko, "Working Wives: The Effects on the Class Structure of the Working Class," *Science and Society* 42, no. 3 (Fall 1978): 257–77; Bureau of the Census, *Statistical Abstract of the United States–1977: National Data Book and Guide to Sources* (Washington, D.C.: U.S. Department of Commerce, Bureau of the Census).

69. *Work in America, Report of a Special Task Force to the Secretary of Health, Education and Welfare* (Cambridge, Mass.: M.I.T. Press, 1973).

70. F. L. Mott and D. Shapiro, "Some Dimensions of Work-Fertility Analysis from the NLS," paper presented at a joint meeting of the Institute of Mathematical Statistics and the American Statistical Association, Chapel Hill, N.C., April 1977.

71. *Work in America*.

72. Alexis Herman, "Still...Small Change for Black Women," *Ms Magazine*, February 1979; pp. 96–98.

73. Louise Knapp Howe, *Pink Collar Workers* (New York: Avon Books, 1978).

74. *Work in America*.

75. Stanley Aronowitz, *False Promises: The Shaping of American Working Class Consciousness* (New York: McGraw-Hill Book Company, 1973).

76. Carol Tavris and Carole Offir, *The Longest War* (New York: Harcourt Brace Jovanovich, 1977).

77. *Work in America*.

78. Carole Lopate, *Women in Medicine* (Baltimore: Johns Hopkins University Press, 1968).

79. Virginia E. O'Leary, *Toward Understanding Women* (Belmont, Calif.: Wadsworth Publishing Company, 1977).

80. M. Corcoran, "Work Experience, Labor Force Withdrawals, and Women's Empirical Results Using the 1976 Panel Study of Income Dynamics," paper presented at the Conference on Women in the Labor Market, cosponsored by Barnard College and the U.S Department of Labor, New York, September 1977.

81. Barbara Ross, "Women Rip

Firm for 'Pressure' on Sterilization,"
The New York Post, 2 January 1979.

Six: Middle Adulthood

1. Robert E. Schell and Elizabeth
Hall, *Developmental Psychology
Today*, 3 ed. (New York: Random
House, 1979).

2. Daniel J. Levinson, *The Seasons
of a Man's Life* (New York: Alfred A.
Knopf, 1978); Gail Sheehy, *Passages:
Predictable Crises of Adult Life* (New
York: E.P. Dutton, 1974).

3. Bernice L. Neugarten, ed.,
Middle Age and Aging (Chicago:
University of Chicago Press, 1968).

4. Stanley Aronowitz, *False
Promises: The Shaping of American
Working Class Consciousness* (New
York: McGraw-Hill Book Company,
1973); *Work in America, Report of a
Special Task Force to the Secretary
of Health, Education and Welfare*
(Cambridge, Mass.: M.I.T. Press,
1973).

5. Nadine Brozon, "A Study of the
American Man," *The New York
Times*, 12 January 1979.

6. Juanita M. Kreps, *Women and
the American Economy: A Look to
the 1980's* (Englewood Cliffs, N.J.:
Prentice-Hall, 1976).

7. Lillian B. Rubin, *Worlds of
Pain: Life in the Working-Class
Family* (New York: Basic Books,
1976), and Lillian B. Rubin, *Women
of a Certain Age: The Midlife Search
for Self* (New York: Harper & Row,
1979).

8. Susan Romer Kaplan, "The
Resolution of Ambivalence: The
Reentrance of Women Over Age 30
into the University Leading to the
Ph.D., L.L.D., M.B.A., and M.D.
Degrees," unpublished doctoral
dissertation proposal, University of
California, Berkeley, 1979; Jean
Campbell, "Women Drop Back In:
Educational Innovation in the

Sixties," in *Academic Women on the
Move*, eds. A.S. Rossi and A.
Calderwood (New York: Russell Sage
Foundation, 1973), pp. 93–194; K.
Patricia Cross, *Beyond the Open
Door: New Students in Higher
Education* (San Francisco: Jossey-Bass
Publishers, 1971).

9. Rhoda Baruch, "The
Achievement Motive in Women:
Implications for Career
Development," *Journal of Personality
and Social Psychology* 5, no. 3 (1967):
260–7.

10. Neugarten, *Middle Age*;
Orville G. Brim, "Theories of the
Male Mid-Life Crisis," *The
Counseling Psychologist* 6, no. 1
(1976): 2–7.

11. Nancy Frazier and Myra
Sadker, *Sexism in School and Society*
(New York: Harper & Row, 1973);
Kaplan, "The Resolution of
Ambivalence."

12. Project Chance at Brooklyn
College of the City University of
New York and the Center for
Continuing Education of Women at
the University of Michigan are two
examples of the many new programs
designed to facilitate reentry of
women students.

13. Rubin, *Women of a Certain
Age*.

14. Levinson, *The Seasons*.

15. Rubin, *Women of a Certain
Age*.

16. Arthur J. Norton, "The Family
Life Cycle Updated: Components and
Uses," in *Selected Studies in
Marriage and the Family*, eds. R.F.
Winch and G.B. Spanier (New York:
Holt, Rinehart & Winston, 1974), pp.
162–70.

17. Rubin, *Women of a Certain
Age*.

18. Ibid., p. 53.

19. Ibid., p. 123.

20. I. Deutsher, "The Quality of
Postparental Life," in *Middle Age and*

Aging, ed. Neugarten, pp. 263–68.

21. Levinson, *The Seasons.*

22. M. Adams, "The Single Woman in Today's Society: A Reappraisal," *American Journal of Orthopsychiatry* 41 (1971): 776–86.

23. William H. Masters and Virginia E. Johnson, "Emotional Poverty, A Marriage Crisis of the Middle Years," in *The Quality of Life: The Middle Years,* The American Medical Association (Acton, Mass.: Publishing Sciences Group, 1974), pp. 101–8.

24. Mary Jane Sherfey, *The Nature and Evolution of Female Sexuality (New York: Vintage Books, 1973).*

25. Shere Hite, *The Hite Report: A Nationwide Survey of Female Sexuality* (New York: Dell Publishing Co., 1976); Estelle Fuchs, *The Second Season: Life, Love and Sex—Women in the Middle Years* (Garden City, N.Y.: Anchor Press, 1977); Marilyn P. Whitely and Susan B. Poulsen, "Assertiveness and Sexual Satisfaction in Employed Professional Women," *Journal of Marriage and the Family* 37 (1975): 573–81.

26. Hite, *The Hite Report.*

27. Rubin, *Women of a Certain Age.*

28. Sidney Abbott and Barbara Love, *Sappho Was a Right-On Woman: A Liberated View of Lesbianism* (New York: Stein & Day, 1973); Ginny Vida, ed., *Our Right to Love: A Lesbian Resource Book* (Englewood Cliffs, N.J.: Prentice-Hall, 1978); Sasha Gregory Lewis, *Sunday's Women: A Report On Lesbian Life Today* (Boston: Beacon Press, 1979).

29. Neugarten, *Middle Age*; Brim, "Theories of the Male Mid-Life Crisis"; William H. Masters and Virginia E. Johnson, *Human Sexual Inadequacy* (Boston: Little, Brown & Co., 1970).

30. Bernice Neugarten and David L. Guttman, "Age-Sex Roles and Personality in Middle Age: A Thematic Apperception Study," in *Middle Age and Aging,* ed. Neugarten, pp. 58–70.

31. Alan P. Bell and Martin S. Weinberg, *Homosexualities: A Study of Diversity Among Men and Women* (New York: Simon & Schuster, 1978); Jim Kelley, "The Aging Male Homosexual: Myth and Reality," in *Gay Men: The Sociology of Male Homosexuality,* ed. Martin P. Levine (New York: Colophon Books, 1979), pp. 253–62.

32. Rubin, *Women of a Certain Age.*

33. Ibid.

Seven: Later Adulthood

1. Bernice L. Neugarten and David L. Guttman, "Sex Roles and Personality in Middle Age: A Thematic Apperception Study," in *Middle Age and Aging,* ed. Bernice L. Neugarten (Chicago: University of Chicago Press, 1968), pp. 58–70.

2. Nancy Hicks, "Life After 65," in *Focus: Aging, Annual Editions,* ed. Harold Cox (Guilford, Conn.: The Dushkin Publishing Group, 1978), pp. 120–2.

3. Ibid.

4. Ibid.; Carol Stack, *All Our Kin: Strategies for Survival in a Black Community* (New York: Colophon Books, 1974).

5. P. Wingfield Perry, "The Night of Ageism," *Mental Hygiene* 58, no. 3 (Summer 1974): 13–20.

6. J. Wax, "It's Like Your Own Home Here," *The New York Times Magazine,* 21 November 1976.

7. Lewis R. Aiken, *Later Life* (Philadelphia: W. B. Saunders Company, 1978).

8. Elizabeth Kübler-Ross, *On*

Death and Dying (New York: Macmillan Publishing Co., 1969).

9. E. Cumming and W. E. Henry, *Growing Old: The Process of Disengagement* (New York: Basic Books, 1961).

10. H. S. Maas and J. A. Kuypers, *From Thirty to Seventy: A Forty-Year Longitudinal Study of Changing Life Styles and Personal Development* (San Francisco: Jossey-Bass Publishers, 1974).

11. Alan Kerckhoff, "Husband-Wife Expectations and Reactions to Retirement," in *Social Aspects of Aging,* eds. I. H. Simpson and J. C. McKinney (Durham, N.C.: Duke University Press, 1966), pp. 160–72.

12. Aiken, *Later Life.*

13. Hicks, "Life after 65."

14. Bureau of the Census, *Statistical Abstract of the United States—1977: National Data Book and Guide to Sources* (Washington, D.C.: U.S. Department of Commerce, Bureau of the Census, 1977).

15. J. Bernardo, "Survivorship and Social Isolation," *The Family Coordinator* 19 (1970): 11–25; H. Z. Lopata, *Widowhood in an American City* (Cambridge, Mass.: Schenkman Publishing Co., 1973); R. E. Schell and E. Hall, *Developmental Psychology Today,* 3 ed. (New York: Random House, 1979).

16. Aiken, *Later Life.*

17. A. Verwoerdt, E. Pfeiffer, and H. Wang, "Sexual Behavior in Senescence: II Patterns of Sexual Activity and Interest," *Geriatrics* 24 (1969): 137–54.

18. Morton Puner, *To the Good Long Life: What We Know About Growing Old* (New York: Universe Books, 1974); William H. Masters and Virginia E. Johnson, *Human Sexual Inadequacy* (Boston: Little, Brown & Company, 1970); Shere Hite, *The Hite Report: A Nationwide Study of Female Sexuality* (New York: Dell Publishing Co., 1976).

Index

Photograph Acknowledgments

Cover: © 1980 by Susan B. Trowbridge. *Frontispiece:* Michael Hardy, Woodfin Camp and Associates. *Pages 2–3:* © 1979 by Mariette Pathy Allen. *Pages 16–17:* Marvin Newman, Woodfin Camp and Associates. *Pages 30–31:* © by Bettye Lane. *Pages 46–47:* © by Michael Weisbrot and Family. *Pages 80–81:* Joan Lifton, Woodfin Camp and Associates. *Pages 110–111:* © 1978 by Joel Gordon. *Pages 124–125:* J. Berndt, Stock/Boston.

This book was composed in Trump and Olive Antique by Weinglas Typography Company, Port Washington, New York. It was printed and bound by R.R. Donnelley & Sons Company, Chicago, Illinois. The covers were printed by Algen Press, Queens, New York.

WOMEN'S LIVES WOMEN'S WORK

ABOUT
The Sex-Role Cycle
Socialization from Infancy to Old Age

The Sex-Role Cycle, by Nancy Romer, clearly describes the forces that encourage males and females to become masculine and feminine. Based on research from many disciplines, this concise overview is enriched with lively examples from important studies. Romer examines the developing individual and takes a close look at the central agents of socialization in each period of life. Her chapters on adolescence, adulthood, and old age offer fresh insights into socialization as a lifelong process. Viewing people not only as victims of socialization, but also as partners in the process, Romer considers the possibilities for changing sex roles in order to improve the lives of women and men. She avoids overgeneralization and illuminates the complex elements—gender, race, ethnicity, age, and social class—that intersect to define an individual. Illustrated with photographs.

The Feminist Press   0-912670-69-X

McGraw-Hill   0-07-020425-X